Stock Markets Are For You Too

Basic Concepts & Terminology

Fundamental Analysis

Technical Analysis

Picking Winning Stocks

Tax Implications

Joy of Giving Back

SUSHIL BALI

DEDICATION

dedicated to

my parents

&

grand parents

seeking their blessings from

wherever they are

CONTENTS

Foreword vi

Acknowledgements viii

Introduction ix

1 Basic Stock Market Concepts & Terminology 1

2 Entities Supporting Stock Trading 13

3 Basic Rules of General & Stock Market Investing 20

4 Trading Strategies 24

5 Fundamental Analysis: Economy & Industry 30

6 What to Read in Annual Reports of Companies 35

7 Qualitative Analysis of a Company 38

8 Quantitative Analysis: Financial Statements 40

9 Quantitative Analysis: Financial Ratios 70

10 Calculating Intrinsic Value of a Stock 84

11 Picking Winning Stocks for Investing 94

12 Candlesticks & Candlestick Charts 101

13 Volume, Resistance & Support Levels 114

14 Lagging & Leading Indicators 117

15 Fibonacci Retracements & The Dow Theory 125

16 Risk to Reward Ratio 134

17 Picking Winning Stocks for Trading 136

18 Tax Implications on Dividends & Selling Stocks 139

19 The Joy of Giving Back 145

Foreword

"History provides a crucial insight regarding market crisis: they are inevitable, painful and ultimately surmountable"

Shelby M C Davis

If you are looking for wealth creation, investing in stocks should be an essential part of your financial planning / strategy.

Investing in stock markets is considered to be a 'high risk, high reward' option. Therefore, it is sometimes called 'satta bazar,' literally meaning a market for gambling, as many investors invest their money with little understanding that is based on tips from friends, colleagues, business magazines, or listening to experts on television channels or simply following other lucky investors.

This methodology must change, thanks largely to IT that provides all the necessary required data to the investor in real time, and if one knows how to interpret it, one can change a gamble into a well-considered investment. This practical and easily comprehensible book does just that for you.

The book in well-articulated twenty chapters takes the reader through the process of stock selection, so that an investor can invest wisely. The author begins by explaining basic concepts and commonly used terms in stock market discussions in a simple narrative form so that it is easily understood by anyone, even by persons who have no finance background. It is then followed by elaborate explanations on how to carry out fundamental and technical analysis of stocks. You will also learn how to read and interpret financial statements of companies, calculate financial ratios and intrinsic value of stocks, analyse technical charts and pick winning stocks for investing. Included in the book are various check lists which a reader can use while analysing stocks so that nothing is left out.

When we profit we have to pay taxes. Therefore, as an investor you must understand the tax implications when you sell stocks.

Reading the book will enable you to invest wisely knowing when to buy what, what to keep and when to sell what.

LT GEN MAHESH VIJ (RETD), PVSM, AVSM

March 2021

ACKNOWLEDGMENTS

my sincere gratitude to

my dear wife, Manju

my two lovely daughters, Swati & Priyanka

my two sons in law, Veshal & Sarat

for assisting me during the writing of this book

&

Lt Gen Mahesh Vij

for motivating me to write this book

&

all my teachers

for all that I am today

&

friends and colleagues

for believing in me

Introduction

"Everyone has the power to follow the stock markets. If you made it through fifth grade, you can do it"

Peter Lynch

My earlier book, 'BE YOUR OWN FINANCIAL ADVISOR' was published in September of 2020 which has been well received and appreciated. The book is available through Amazon in both formats, paperback as well as an e-book. In India, the paperback version is also available through Notion Press.

I strongly believe that investment does not start and end with buying a financial product. It is a journey that starts with:

1. Learning investing basics,

2. Planning an investment strategy based on goals,

3. Knowing, understanding and choosing the right investment product for each of the goals,

4. Creating a protection ring around your created assets, including self and family,

5. Understanding tax implications and how to reduce the tax burden, and finally

6. Seeing that the wealth you create is passed on safely to desired beneficiaries.

'BE YOUR OWN FINANCIAL ADVISOR' was written with the above objectives in mind and the aim of making my reader an 'informed investor' by introducing to him or her the various available investment avenues with a clear message that they should invest only in a product that they understand. For beginners, I strongly recommend that they read this book before reading this one.

Amongst the various investment avenues that were discussed in that book, I had introduced my readers to the option of investing in stock markets directly. At the same time, I had warned them of the dangers of investing in markets without adequate knowledge. So, to arm my readers with the required knowledge, I decided to write this book in a simple language, explaining basic concepts, that will give the investor the required confidence to go ahead, invest and benefit from the stock markets without fear.

With the prevailing low interest rates, traditional products like fixed deposits or post office schemes, etc are no longer attractive. It is only that while investing in stock markets that you can beat inflation and grow your wealth.

There are two ways to invest in stock markets, one is through the mutual funds and the second is through direct equity. Therefore, the first logical question that comes to mind is, why invest in direct equity when the mutual fund route is available?

There is no doubt that there are several advantages of investing in mutual funds over direct equity. Mutual funds reduce risk by investing in a number of stocks. You can invest in them with much less money, with little involvement of time and effort from your end. Since the mutual fund AMC is doing all the work for you, the cost of investing in mutual funds is more than investing in direct equity.

Direct equity investing requires some expertise, time and effort from your side. Investing in it is riskier when compared to investing in mutual funds but it is more rewarding. It is primarily for this reason that people invest directly in stocks. To give you an idea, the S&P BSE Sensex index gave trailing returns of 114.30%, 15.37% and 10.54% over the last 3, 5 and 10 years respectively. Against this, generally mutual funds have given a little better return. However, if one would have invested, for example, directly in HDFC Bank the rewards would have been 17.82%, 24.53% and 21.28% over 3, 5 and 10 years respectively. Similarly, TCS gave returns of 24.63%,

20.58% and 18.12%. I have given the example of stocks that have beaten the Sensex, but it is not true for all stocks in the Sensex, for example, ITC gave returns of (-)7.11%, (-) 0.15% and 6.13%. Therefore, choosing right stocks is important.

Another reason, why people invest directly in stocks is because stocks offer dividends in addition to capital appreciation. However, the dominating factor while choosing stocks should always be capital appreciation and not dividends.

People, by and large, fear stock markets because of a few myths that surround them. Let us analyse each myth one by one.

Myth No 1: Markets are Very Risky

Investing in stock markets is very risky, is the most dominating myth in people's mind. I agree with them to a little extent but disagree to a large extent because markets are undoubtedly risky when you invest in them without adequate knowledge and understanding. They are risky when you invest in them for short periods thinking of making a quick buck. They are risky when you invest based on tips and leads from relatives, friends, brokers, colleagues, etc who themselves do not understand stock markets or listening to anchors and experts on television business channels who may have vested interests not in line with yours. You should, therefore, suspect all such advice. When you invest based on any such advice, you are only speculating and are bound to reap losses. Remember, it is your money, and no one can take care of it more than you yourself.

Investing in stock markets is risky if you trade in stocks, but if you invest in them, after obtaining sufficient knowledge, careful analysis, research and skill, you reduce risk to a very large extent.

Stock markets work on the concept of buying and selling contracts. Therefore, some have to lose for some to win. Remember that as a retail investor you are pitted against market participants that include big domestic and foreign institutional investors. These market participants have access to market information, tons of money and backing of fulltime very qualified professionals. I can assure you that you will always end up losing money, losing confidence and the experience will not allow you to ever return to markets again. Speculative investors can be equated to gamblers, and we all know what happened to Yudhishthira when he gambled recklessly against the expert Shakuni.

The Sensex has been in existence since 1875. It was only on 1 April 1979 that this index based on 30 listed well established companies with a base value of 100 was established. During its journey of 41 years, there have been several ups and downs and periods of consolidation. It was on 25 July 1990, that is after 11 years, the index touched the four-digit figure for the first time and closed at 1,001. It crossed the next 3,000 points in less than a year and the markets then dropped because of the Harshad Mehta scam that led to the closure of the Bombay Stock Exchange for a month and the creation of the National Stock Exchange.

In the budget announcements of 1991-92 some major reforms were pushed through which led to liberalisation in investment and trade regimes fostering greater competition and efficiency. The Sensex reached 5,000 in 1999 and 10,000 in 2006. In 2008, the sub-prime crisis hit the US markets and the Sensex dropped to 8,500. The markets saw the 2009 Satyam scam.

After the second round of reforms in 2012, the Sensex grew steadily in spite of the huge fall witnessed in March 2020 because of the Covid-19 pandemic, and is now, as I write in the first week of February 2021, trading above the 50,000 mark.

Markets have witnessed and overcome several crisis created by Yes Bank, IL&FS, DHFL, the stockbroker Ketan Parekh etc. The recent Covid-19 pandemic spread panic amongst investors because of country wide lock down that sent the Sensex crashing in March of 2020 by as much as 23.1%, and several stocks tumbling by as much as 40 to 70%, causing destruction of over Rs 14.6 lakh crore of wealth. All this happened in just two weeks. Similar phenomenon was experienced in stock markets all around the world. However, stock markets crashes are great buying opportunities. Astute investors who can smell the incoming crashes in its early stage, redeem their investments and reinvest after the crash.

Soon after the markets fell to new lows, they also started recovering rapidly, and in a short span of ten months, as I write, the Sensex is at an all-time high of 50,731 (5 Feb 2021) and several stocks are trading beyond their

52 weeks highs. From a bear market in March 2020, the market is now in a bull market!

So, it is seen that if you remain invested for longer durations in the right stocks, the markets can be extremely rewarding in spite of scams, sell offs during natural and un-natural events, the pandemic and the periods of volatility.

Myth No 2: No Background in Finance

The other myth is that it is very difficult for individuals to understand financial statements, financial ratios, etc if they don't have a background in finance. Certainly, a background in finance helps, but again this myth is true to a little extent only as there are several bigtime successful investors in India and abroad who have made huge fortunes without a background in finance. It only takes a little effort to understand all that is necessary to invest in markets. What you really need is tons of passion, patience and common sense.

Myth No 3: Large Companies Don't Give Good Returns

Again, some would argue that you cannot earn big money when you invest in well-established and large companies. None of this is really true. There are several big companies that have created huge wealth for investors. Over the last 25 years, the biggest wealth creators have been Reliance Industries, Hindustan Unilever and Infosys.

Myth No 4: You Need Lots of Money to Invest in Stock Markets

You really don't need a large amount of money to start investing. As a matter of fact, you should begin investing in direct equity with little money and then scale up slowly after you gain experience and confidence. There are several free websites that offer information freely for your research.

Myth No 5: High Risk means High Returns

Although risk and returns are related, but this relationship cannot be assumed to be correct all the time. If this relationship was true, then everyone would be trading in high-risk instruments only.

Myth No 6: Bluechip Stocks are Safe

Well, this can be true to a large extent, but this is not always true. There are several stocks that were favourites and considered to be good quality stocks have eroded investor's wealth almost completely, for example, Reliance Communications, Suzlon, Reliance Capital, Reliance Infrastructure, Jaiprakash Industries, Unitech, etc. Therefore, you cannot just buy good quality stocks and sleep over thinking that if you remain invested in them you will generate huge returns. Instead, you must review your portfolio regularly so that you can take appropriate actions well in time.

Myth No 7: Long Term Investing Generate Good Returns

People who have succeeded in stock markets are people who have followed and mastered the strategy of picking good quality stocks at reasonable price points and remained invested in them so long the stock did not violate the criteria of remaining a good quality stock. Holding on to stocks over long periods that begin to under-perform or show signs of perishing returns may not be a good idea. So, believing blindly in long term investing, can be dangerous.

Disruption Effects: Good & Bad

With advancements in technology, natural and unnatural calamities, changing lifestyles, work cultures and changing individual preferences, businesses are susceptible to frequent disruptions.

I recall that it was in 1996 that mobile communications in India started with pagers and some giant companies invested heavily in the hope of providing mobile communications through satellites. In 1997, mobile telephone operators launched their services and drove out the paging companies and the satellite communication providers nipped their project even before they could launch their services as they realised that they would not be able to compete with mobile telephony. Both companies suffered huge losses.

A few years back, Maruti stock crashed because of prolonged labour unrest that led to lower production and lower profits for the company.

There was a time in India when every second person carried a Nokia mobile handset. Today this brand is nowhere to be seen. Similarly, so many well-known brands have disappeared as they could not keep pace with the changes that were taking place around them.

Internet penetration has been another big disruptor. It changed the way many companies and individuals worked. It has enhanced efficiency in the working of many companies, but it has also affected profitability of several companies adversely. Today, you can do several jobs sitting at home all by yourself. If you wish to shop, pay bills, invest or trade in stocks, etc you can do through the net, unlike the earlier days where you were dependant on the physical services.

The recent Covid-19 pandemic has changed the way we live and work. The pandemic saw the lockdown in almost all major cities around the world and the breakdown of medical resources resulting in more than two and a half million deaths. The pandemic has been a great disruption providing several opportunities to many industries as well as harming many.

We see a decrease in demand for commercial and living rental spaces, decrease in consumption of petrol, as many people are allowed to work from home. Shopping patterns have changed, with many preferring to shop online. The bus, rail and air travel and the hotel industry have been hit hard because of restrictions imposed on travel. The insurance industry has gained as people have now understood the impact of huge hospital bills on their savings when they are not insured. Health care and hygiene product providers gained.

During the pandemic, some people lost jobs, some received pay cuts and some businesses had to even shut down. These can lead to serious payment defaults.

China is the manufacturing hub of the world and due to the pandemic supplies got disrupted. Therefore, the world felt the need to reduce dependency on China. India could be a big beneficiary of this.

On its part, to reduce dependency on other nations, the government of India announced the Made in India and the Atmanirbhar (self-reliant) campaigns and to give it a boost the Production Linked Incentive (PLI) scheme. You can invest in such companies that stand to benefit from these announcements.

The introduction of electrical vehicles as alternative to traditional vehicles run on petrol and diesel will be the next big disrupter for oil and gas companies and rid the nation of huge oil bill payments in foreign currency. Therefore, exciting times are ahead.

So, we see that disruptions are good for some and bad for others. As investors, we should be able to foresee disruptions and align our investment strategy accordingly by buying into companies that are probable beneficiaries of a disruption and move out of companies that could be hurt.

Relation Between Equities & Bonds

Now a few words on bonds. Companies raise money either through issue of shares or corporate bonds and the government raises capital through bonds that are issued through the Reserve Bank of India. Bonds are considered safer investments compared to stocks as they carry considerably less risk. As investors we must understand the relationship between equities and bonds.

Interest rates and inflation in the economy are two key factors that determine bond yields. As inflation rises, interest rates also rise. Rise or fall in interest rates affect bond prices and bond yields. When interest rates rise, bond prices fall but bond yields rise, and when interest rates fall, bond prices rise but bond yields fall. Therefore, investors of stock markets keep a watch on interest rates which are regulated by the Reserve Bank of India so as to strategise investment plans accordingly.

Bond yields are inversely proportional to return on equities. When bond yields begin to rise investors start reallocating their investments from equities to bonds as the opportunity cost of investing in equities goes up thereby making them less attractive.

The increase in bond yields also increases the cost of raising capital that has an effect on its earnings and the resultant reduction in its price value.

When there is mass selling of bonds, the stock markets witness a slide.

Rising bond yields upset the government's spending programme as it borrows at a higher rate which has a direct impact on the nation's real economy. In addition, the government's borrowing rate is used as benchmark for pricing loans to corporates.

When bond yields rise in the US or developed countries, there is an outflow of investments from emerging markets like India leading to a fall in our markets.

With the budget announcements on 1 Feb 2021, RBI will now allow retail participation in government bonds also called G-secs. As individual investors you should be watchful before deciding to invest in them.

Investor or Trader

People around the world who have made enormous wealth through stock markets have been investors and not traders. I, therefore, appeal to my readers that if you wish to make big gains in stock markets you must invest in stocks and not trade. I have included chapters on technical analysis only to help you to make buy and sell decisions and not to motivate you to trade.

Although there are six chapters on Technical Analysis, they are not enough to make you a good trader in stocks. If you wish to become one, I suggest that you do more research on the subject.

Best Time to Invest in Stocks

The best time to buy stocks is when the markets are in a bear phase when they trade at or near their intrinsic values or when deep corrections occur in the markets. These opportunities occur off and on, one has to be patient like a hunter who waits for his prey.

Building a Portfolio

A portfolio with about 15 to 20 good stocks is quite manageable by individual investors. Anything more may be difficult to handle. To reduce risk to your portfolio, your basket of stocks should be well diversified. Diversification can be achieved by investing in stocks across trending sectors as well as not being unduly overweight on any one stock within a sector.

How Much to Invest in Direct Equity?

There are several investment avenues available to individual investors. Your choice of which instrument to invest in must be in line with your various goals as listed out in your financial plan. Investment in direct equity should preferably be against your goal of wealth creation and not any other goal. If that be so, each person depending on his resources and risk appetite must estimate as to how much he or she should allocate to this. There can be no one rule that can fit all.

When to Sell Stocks

There are many people who easily sell their best performing stocks since they become profitable and hang on with their losers in the hope that someday they would recover their original cost. On the contrary, we should hold on to our best performing stocks and get rid of our loss-making ones quickly before losses increase. A good stock must be sold only when it stops meeting the criteria which prompted you to buy it.

Bull Markets

Bull markets are situations caused by 20% increase in stock prices usually after a drop of 20% and before a second decline of 20%. This is the most common definition. Bear markets are just the opposite. Bull markets take place when the economy is strengthening.

There are four phases in a bull market: expansion, peak, contraction and trough. However, it is difficult to predict the start of bull runs or its peak before the contraction phase begins. A bull phase may run into a few months or even a few years.

People employ different strategies for buying stocks in a bull market. Investors take advantage of bull markets by buying stocks early and selling them when they peak out. Another way could be buying into dips that occur frequently or adding into your already bought shares that are on the rise.

Bull markets tempt many people to join the party. There is no harm in doing so as some easy money can be made during this phase but remember that this phase is not for buying good quality stocks as their prices would be well beyond their intrinsic value.

Many people who don't have any understanding of markets happen to make money during a bull run and start assuming that they have become experts without realising that it is the market that gave them the profits and they had little role to play. During a bull market phase, people trade in stocks and not invest in them.

New Challenges

Many analysts depend on how the markets behaved historically but markets have their own way of surprising even the most experienced and successful investors. Guessing what the markets will do, is not easy as new and new challenges get thrown up, some through domestic and some through international issues, some because of natural or unnatural causes. Some of these challenges can be foreseen and can be addressed easily. The ones that are impossible to predict are the ones that cause maximum havoc.

Mistakes are Normal

In your journey of buying and selling stocks, you will make mistakes. No one has ever had 100% success. Mistakes are part and parcel of this game as markets will throw up new challenges very often. It is important to acknowledge mistakes and learn from them.

Advice for Beginners

As a beginner, you should start investing in direct equity slowly. As you gain experience, you can get more aggressive but never reckless. Remember the old saying, never put all your eggs in one basket. Always have a diversified portfolio that have allocations to direct equity, equity mutual funds, debt instruments, gold, real estate, etc based on your overall financial plan and risk profile.

Few Important Points to Remember

1. Good stocks will always beat markets and generate wealth.

2. There are only a few good stocks that everyone wishes to buy which leads to their high valuations.

3. Consistent wealth can be generated by companies that have a quality business that generate a steady earnings growth of 10% to 20% over a ten-year period and when acquired at reasonable valuations.

4. Financials will always be an important sector for growth of any economy.

5. Companies leap frogging from Small caps to Large caps are rare. However, a fair number of them move to the Mid cap category but these need to be identified early from a large base.

6. Best high performing stocks are available within the stocks that are listed 101 to 250 by market capitalisation.

7. Quite a few midcaps have generated wealth but at the same time several have gone oblivion because of poor management quality. Hence, be cautious when investing in midcaps.

8. Stocks whose PEG valuation is less than one, tend to significantly outperform the market.

9. Stocks with less than ten P/E almost invariably outperform.
10. Price / Book or Price / Sales ratios of less than 1 are useful metrics for significant out performance.

The Book

There are several books written by experts and eminent personalities on stock market investing. However, I find that most of them offer unworkable complicated theories which confuses the ordinary investor. This book promises to make the reader an informed and intelligent investor in the stock market. There are no promises of turning you into a billionaire overnight. The book has been written in simple language, explaining basic concepts such that can be easily understood by beginners as well as those who have been investing with little or no knowledge of markets.

The nineteen chapters in the book can be divided into four segments for ease of understanding:

1. **Segment 1:** This segment has four introductory chapters. The first chapter explains the basic terminology that is used by stock market experts and analysts, the understanding of which is essential for any investor to be successful. The second chapter talks about the two stock exchanges, role and functions of SEBI as the regulating body, influence of RBI's fiscal policy on our investment decisions, and the support provided by SEBI registered brokers. General and basic rules of stock market investing are enumerated in the third chapter. The various trading strategies that an investor or trader can employ are discussed in the fourth chapter.

2. **Segment 2:** This segment covers the important subject of how fundamental analysis helps in analysing which stocks to invest in and at what price. The segment is divided into seven chapters. The first chapter of this segment explains the importance of economy and industry analysis and how it is to be done. The next five chapters cover how a company can be qualitatively and quantitatively analysed through the company's annual reports, and how it's intrinsic value can be calculated so that an investor can choose the right stock to buy at the right price. The last chapter in this segment explains how to pick winning stocks and use a check list where you can summarise all the findings and inferences from your fundamental analysis.

3. **Segment 3:** Although I do not encourage retail investors to trade in stocks, I have included details of how stocks can be technically analysed so that as investors you can use this knowledge to make buy and sell decisions appropriately. This segment has six chapters, the first five chapters explain how candlestick charts and technical indicators can be read and interpreted, how resistance and support levels for stocks can be found, and evaluation of risk to reward ratio while buying stocks for shorter durations. The last chapter in this segment suggests a check list that can be used for summarising the technical analysis inferences.

4. **Segment 4:** This final segment has just two but important chapters. The first chapter explains the tax implications when you sell stocks, and the second is on the joy that you earn when you give back a portion of what you have earned.

I am sure that my readers will benefit immensely by going through the contents of this book and invest in direct equity without fear by following the concepts and principles that have been laid down.

I have enjoyed writing this book and hope my readers will draw immense benefits from it by creating wealth for themselves and their family. That will give me immense satisfaction, happiness and pride.

1 BASIC STOCK MARKET CONCEPTS & TERMINOLOGY

"It's never too late to learn"

Malcolm Forbes

Learning must be built on a strong foundation, so we will start with the basics. To understand stock markets, you need to understand some basic concepts and terms which you will often hear or read. Instead of just giving definitions, I will try and explain the terms through narration in a simple language. The terms that are widely used and need understanding have been written in capital letters.

Journey from a Private to a Public Company

Let us say a person all alone or a group of people start a company, SKB PVT LTD, by pooling some CAPITAL (money) equally or in some proportion. Such a person or a group of people are called PROMOTERS as they are the ones who have started the company. Since they have invested their money in the company, they also become SHAREHOLDERS in the company and, therefore, will own SHARES in proportion to their investment.

In the above story, assuming that there are three promoters, two of them invest Rs 1,00,000 each and the third one Rs 50,000. Against their proportional investment, the company will issue shares to the three promoters. These shares will have a FACE VALUE. The promoters can decide on the face value of each share, say in this case they decide the face value as Rs 10 per share. Then the first two promoters will get 10,000 shares each since they have invested Rs 1,00,000 each, and the third one will get 5,000 because he has invested Rs 50,000. Total shares held by the three promoters are 25,000. Going forward all profits and losses would be shared by the three promoters in proportion to their investments or shares held by them.

If the company makes a profit of say Rs 1,00,000 in the first year, it may decide to distribute the profit within themselves or reinvest the profit in their company. In case they decide to share the profit within themselves, then the profit accruing against each share would be Rs 1,00,000/25,000 that is Rs 4 per share which is called DIVIDEND. The first two promoters would get Rs 10,000x4 that is Rs 40,000 each and the third promoter will get Rs 5,000x4 that is Rs 20,000. Remember dividend is always paid on the face value of each share.

As the company performs well and as time goes by, more and more individuals pour money into the company, and since they are also contributing money into the company, they also become shareholders. A time comes when number of shareholders is more than 200. At this stage, as per company law, the company cannot remain a private limited company and it mandatorily has to get converted into a public limited company. So now our SKB Pvt Ltd company will get converted to SKB Ltd company. Since it is now a public company it can have many shareholders. The shares held by promoters or shareholders are in PHYSICAL FORM and cannot be traded in the markets.

Journey from a Public Company to a Listed Company

Our company is growing well and after a few years, the company wishes to expand its business for which it requires huge capital. This capital can be raised either by taking a loan from Banks or some financial institutions or through public participation.

Let us say that SKB Ltd decides to raise capital through public participation. For this the company will have to sell shares of its company to the public through an IPO (INITIAL PUBLIC OFFER) which is a

PRIMARY MARKET (also called the New Issues Market) transaction as the transaction is between the company and the investors.

The IPO process is complicated and is regulated by the SECURITIES & EXCHANGE BOARD OF INDIA (SEBI) which is the regulatory body in India. Followings steps are necessary to be taken by the company wishing to go for an IPO:

1. The company will hire a team of underwriters or investment banks who will provide guidance in planning the complete IPO process.

2. The company and the underwriters submit the registration statement to SEBI which includes all the financial details and plans of how the company will utilise the money that it will receive.

3. After SEBI approves the registration statement, the next step is to prepare an initial or draft prospectus called a RED HERRING DOCUMENT. This document contains the estimated price of each share with all other details of the IPO with the aim to test waters with potential investors. The promoters and other shareholders are already holding shares with a face value of Rs 10, but the company will not offer the shares at Rs 10 to the public. Say, they offer shares to the public at Rs 18, then the PREMIUM is Rs 8 per share. Premium is required to be paid by the new shareholders because the company has now established itself and the risk for them is much lower than what it was when the promoters set out.

4. Two weeks before the IPO goes public, the company sends its executives to potential investors, normally QUALIFIED INSTITUTIONAL INVESTORS (QIBs) to explain them the benefits of investing in the IPO. QIBs are investors who are presumed to have expertise in evaluating and investing in capital markets.

5. Based on the feedback, the company in consultation with underwriters decide on the price of shares to be offered. Company can float a FIXED PRICE IPO that will have a fixed price per share or a BOOK BUILDING IPO that offers shares at a price band or range.

6. The IPO is advertised for the general public and on a planned date the prospectus and APPLICATION FORMS are made available for investors. Based on the offer, RETAIL INDIVIDUAL INVESTORS (RII), HIGH NET-WORTH INDIVIDUALS (HNI), DOMESTIC INSTITUTIONAL INVESTORS (DII) and FOREIGN INSTITUTIONAL INVESTORS or FOREIGN PORTFOLIO INVESTORS (FII/FPI) apply for these shares. Any individual who applies for shares in an IPO for total value not exceeding Rs two lakhs falls under the category of FII. If an individual applies for shares exceeding Rs two lakhs, he will be considered as HNI. Institutions like banks, insurance companies, mutual funds who invest are considered as DII. Similarly, foreign institutions are called FII or FPI. While applying for shares, company receives money from investors as per the number of shares applied by them.

7. The price of each share is finalised, if the IPO was floated with a book building process. If the issue was fully subscribed, everyone gets shares as per their application. However, if the issue is OVER SUBSCRIBED, which is generally the case, then the company and stake holders sit down on how many shares each one should get. Shares are then issued in DEMATERIALISED form to all eligible investors into their DEMAT ACCOUNT and refunds are credited directly into the investor's bank account if no shares are issued. All this is done within one week of receiving money from investors.

In case you think that it is worthwhile to invest in an IPO, you can apply online or offline. For applying online, you need a TRADING PLATFORM, a DEMAT ACCOUNT and a BANK SAVINGS ACCOUNT which can be provided by your broker. A trading platform is required for buying and selling shares, a demat account is your depository where all your shares that you buy are stored in electronic form, and it is through your bank's savings account that you pay for shares you buy as well as receive credit when you sell shares.

After the shares are allotted to investors, the company then gets the shares LISTED on the STOCK EXCHANGES within three working days. The company may decide to list on the BOMBAY STOCK EXCHANGE (BSE) or the NATIONAL STOCK EXCHANGE (NSE) or both. Once the company is listed on the stock exchanges, the shares of the company can be traded. This market is called the SECONDARY MARKET or the Stock Market. Here the transactions are through investors who wish to buy and sell shares through the stock exchanges.

On listing investors expect the share to trade at a higher value than what they had paid but this may not happen in all cases. The price at which a share is now traded is called MARKET VALUE of the share.

Buying & Selling Shares

For buying and selling shares, an individual needs three things:

1. A Bank Savings Account,

2. A Trading Account, and

3. A Demat account.

Your money in the Bank will help you to buy shares as also receive credit when you sell shares. Buying and selling of shares is done through the trading account, and the shares to your credit are stored in the demat account in electronic form.

It is not necessary to have all the above three accounts from a single source, but it is preferable to have your trading and demat accounts from a single source. There is also no restriction on the number of such accounts that you can hold.

To open these accounts, you will need to fill in a form and submit it to your Bank / Broker with copies of your PAN Card, address proof (driving license, Aadhar card, passport, etc), passport size photograph. In addition, a six-month bank statement or a personalised cancelled cheque may be required if you are not opening your demat or trading account with your bank.

Now that the company, SKB Ltd, is listed on BSE and NSE, the company's shares can be traded on BSE or NSE through the trading platform offered by BROKERS as we cannot buy and sell shares directly on the Stock Exchanges. Both the exchanges operate for trading, Monday to Friday (except holidays), and open at 0900 hours and close at 1530 hours each of these days. This time period between 0900 hours to 1530 hours is called MARKET HOURS.

The first 15 minutes, that is from 0900 to 0915 hours, is called PRE-OPENING MARKET SESSION and this period has been introduced to avoid VOLATILITY or abnormal fluctuations in the share prices. The first eight minutes are used for collecting buy and sell orders and during this time orders can be modified or cancelled. The next four minutes are used for matching the collected orders, and during this time orders cannot be cancelled or modified. The last three minutes are used in facilitating transition from pre-open to normal market session. Pre-opening session gives an indication on which way the market will open.

Once the pre-opening session is over, the CONTINUOUS TRADING SESSION begins from 0915 to 1530 hours. If the markets INDICES (Sensex or Nifty) open higher than the previous day's closing, it is called a GAP UP OPENING. If the markets open lower, then it is called a GAP DOWN OPENING. Similarly, if the stock price opens higher or lower it would be called gap up or gap down opening for the relevant stock.

The price at which the share opens at the beginning of the continuous trading session is called the OPENING PRICE, the price at which the share is last traded at any moment during the time when the market is active is called the LATEST TRADED PRICE. The latest traded price keeps changing and it may or may not be the same on both the exchanges which may be due to unevenness in demand and supply of that particular share. The price at which the last trade is made for the day is called its CLOSING PRICE.

BLOCK DEAL TRADING SESSION is from 0915 to 0950 hours (35 minutes). Block deals are for buy or sell orders with minimum of five lakh shares or minimum value of five crores. Such deals are made by institutional investors.

The period from 1530 to 1540 hours is used by the exchanges for calculating closing prices, and the time from 1540 to 1600 hours is used for execution of trades at closing price. Therefore, you will see little variation in the price of a share or STOCK at 1530 hours and 1600 hours.

Buy and sell orders can be placed after 1600 hours till 0900 hours the next day. Such orders are called AFTER MARKET HOURS ORDERS. However, these orders are executed only after 0915 hours during the normal continuous trading session.

On your trading platform, you will see a lot of data that can help you in deciding at which price you should buy or sell a particular share. You will see the following on the pop-up screen after you have typed in the name of the company in the search field:

1. Name of the SCRIPT or share

2. Number of buy and sell orders, number of shares against each buy and sell order and the price quoted by the buyer and seller

3. Last traded price

4. The price at which the share opened for trade today and the closing price of yesterday

5. Today's highest and lowest price

6. Total number of shares buyers wish to buy, and sellers wish to sell

7. Average traded price for the day

8. Total VOLUME or number of shares that are traded today

9. 52 WEEK HIGH & LOW, that is during the period of last 52 weeks what was the highest and lowest price the share was sold

10. Face value of the share

11. LOWER CIRCUIT (LC) and UPPER CIRCUIT (UC) for the share

The above data is real time, and you can keep refreshing it to see the latest. The data for BSE and NSE will be different as share prices at any moment are decided on the basis of demand and supply of that particular share on that particular exchange. If the demand is more and supply is less, the price of that share will go up. Alternately, if the demand is low and supply is more, the price will fall.

The stock exchanges mark lower and upper circuits for shares with the aim of reducing volatility in the sale of shares. Normally, most stocks have a lower and upper circuit of 20%. So, if the price of a share was Rs 100 at previous day's closing, it can be sold at a minimum price of Rs 80 and a maximum price of Rs 120 for the day. When a stock hits UC, it will have only buyers and no sellers, and if the stock hits LC then it will have only sellers and no buyers.

After you have analysed the pop-up screen on your trading platform you can decide to buy or sell your shares. Since there is a difference in the buying or selling prices between the two exchanges, you can choose to trade either through the BSE or the NSE.

After filling in the quantity that you wish to buy or sell, you will have to specify your trading mode, that is CASH, MARGIN, INTRA DAY, E-MARJIN, COVER, etc. In case you wish to take delivery of shares, you will choose CASH. For other modes we shall discuss in subsequent chapters.

Buy and sell orders are either MARKET or LIMIT orders. If you opt for the market order, your buy or sell order would be executed at the prevailing rate at that moment. If you opt for the limit order, you will have to specify the amount at which you wish to buy or sell, and your order would be executed only at the amount specified by you.

Once you have filled all details, you can click on the BUY or SELL button and you confirm your order, you will see the status on the ORDER BOOK page of your trading platform. Once the order is executed, details will show up in the TRADE BOOK page.

When you buy or sell shares, your broker will issue you a CONTRACT NOTE which is nothing else but a receipt for the transaction. It is mandatory for every broker to issue this note within 24 hours of the transaction. To receive these contract notes you must register your mobile number and e-mail id with your broker. The contract note gives all details of the transaction including the BROKERAGE and other dues like Security Transaction Tax (STT), Goods and Service Tax (GST), Stamp Duty, Exchange Transaction Charges and SEBI Turnover Fees. Brokerage and other charges are required to be paid each time you buy or sell shares. We shall talk about this in more detail later.

When you buy or sell shares, settlement takes place after T+2 days. This means that if you buy a stock today (T day or Trade day), then you would get the shares in your demat account on T+2 working days. In case you have sold shares, you would get money credited into your bank account on T+2 days. The day on which you received the shares in your demat account or cash in your bank account is called the SETTLEMENT DATE.

When you sell shares you will either make a profit or a loss. Such profit or loss is called CAPITAL GAIN or CAPITAL LOSS. As per current tax laws, if you sell your stocks after a holding period of one year, the profit or loss then would be called LONG-TERM CAPITAL GAINS or LONG-TERM CAPITAL LOSS. If you decide to sell your shares before the expiry of one year of holding, the profit or loss would be called SHORT-TERM CAPITAL GAINS or SHORT-TERM CAPITAL LOSS. We shall discuss this in more detail in a separate chapter.

Board of Directors

Every public limited company must have at least three Directors, a private limited company must have a minimum of two, and single owned company at least one on their Board of Directors. The maximum number of Directors a company can have is fifteen. However, a company can have more than fifteen directors by passing a special resolution in a general body meeting.

Directors are considered as trustees of the company's assets and are responsible for directing, controlling and managing the affairs of the company. An individual can be a director in a maximum of twenty companies.

It is mandatory that at least one of the directors is a woman, and at least one director who has lived in India for a minimum of 182 calendar days of the previous day. Also, at least one third of the directors should be independent directors. Independent directors are non-executive directors, that is they don't take active part in the day to day running of the company but help the company to improve its credibility and enhance governance standards.

Board Meetings

Every new company must hold its BOARD MEETING within 30 days of its incorporation. Thereafter, it is mandatory to hold at least four meetings in a year. Board meetings are attended only by the board members. These meetings are held to discuss the company's future plans, performance, etc.

Annual General Meeting (AGM) / Extraordinary General Meeting EGM)

An Annual General Body Meeting (AGM) is required to be held every year. This meeting is between the company's DIRECTORS and its shareholders where the directors present the company's ANNUAL REPORT which contains information about the company's performance during the year and its strategy going forward. It is during this meeting when shareholders can vote on important matters such as appointments to the Board of Directors, executive's compensation, dividend payments, selection of auditors, etc. It also offers an opportunity for shareholders to ask questions about the company's performance or future plans. AGMs can be convened only on working days and during working hours only.

A company can also hold an Extraordinary General Meeting (EGM), also called an Emergency or a Special General Meeting that is apart from the Annual General Meeting. An EGM is generally called to discuss an urgent matter that cannot wait till the AGM is convened. Such matters could be removal of an executive or some legal matter that has cropped up and needs urgent attention. An EGM can be convened on any day, including public holidays.

Dividends

When a company makes profit, it may decide to declare a dividend by paying whole or a part of its profits to its shareholders. Such dividends are notified as a percentage and calculated on the face value of the share. These are paid directly into the investor's bank account.

Bonus Shares

If the company is doing well, it may decide to reward its investors by declaring BONUS SHARES for them. If these are announced as 1:2, it means that an investor will get 1 free share for every 2 held by him or her. If the announcement is 2:5, it means that one would get 2 free shares for every 5 held. In all cases the face value of share does not change nor the total value of your investment.

Stock Split

It may also happen that after several years the price of one share of the company touches, say Rs 5,000. Since this share has now become costly fewer stocks are traded on the exchange. To reduce the cost of each share, the company decides to SPLIT the share. If the face value of the share is Rs 10, the company can split its share into two or more parts. In case it decides to split the share into two parts, the new face value of the share would be Rs 5. When a share is split the market value also goes down, but investors don't lose money as they get one additional share for each share they hold, without paying anything extra. Since the market value of each share gets reduced after the split, a greater number of shares are traded each day. A share cannot have a face value of less than Re 1.

Rights Issue

A Rights Issue is an invitation to the company's shareholders to buy additional shares on a pro rata basis at a discounted rate to the market value within a specified time period. This transaction is through the primary market as the shares are issued by the company to its shareholders without the involvement of the stock markets.

Companies announce a Rights Issue to raise additional capital for purposes of paying off debt, expansion, for acquisition of another company or any general corporate purposes.

Shareholders have the option of buying their full or part entitlement of shares or not buying any. They can also apply for additional shares over and above their entitlement as these would be available because some may have decided not to buy at all or buy only part of their entitlement.

Companies prefer to raise capital through a Rights Issue as it is the fastest and cheapest method of raising capital and at the same time also pleases its shareholders by offering shares at a discounted rate.

After the Rights Issue, the number of shares will increase, and its market value will drop.

Shareholders should not blindly opt for buying shares in a Rights Issue but should buy only after careful evaluation of the company's finances, performance and the purpose for which a Rights Issue is being offered.

Important Dates

Three dates are important to understand when dividends, bonus shares, stock splits or rights issue are given by a company. In each of the instances these dates will come into play. To understand their significance, as an example, let us understand these dates in the case of a bonus issue announcement of say 1:2 when the share is trading at Rs 300 per share:

1. **Announcement Date:** This is the date when the company announces that it wishes to give bonus shares to its investors in the ratio of 1 free share for every two held by the investor.

2. **Record Date:** You will be eligible to bonus shares only to the extent you hold shares of that company in your demat account. So, you will get 50 free shares if you have 100 shares of the company in your demat account on this date.

3. **Ex-Bonus Date:** This is the date when the share starts to trade at the revised price. Since the bonus ratio is 1:2, the share price of the stock will fall to Rs 200 or thereabout on this date.

In this chapter, we have discussed several basic concepts and through them the meaning of several terms that are often used while we read or discuss stock markets. However, there are several more which we shall discover as we go along.

2 ENTITIES SUPPORTING STOCK TRADING

"The best way to rob a bank is to own it"

Robert Kiyosaki

There are several entities working in the forefront and background to ensure that investors can buy and sell stocks safely and freely in a transparent environment. Let us see which all entities are involved in this small world, apart from investors and listed companies:

1. Depositories

2. Depository Participants (DPs)

3. Stockbrokers

4. Banks

5. Clearing Corporations

6. Stock & Commodity Exchanges

7. Securities & Exchange Board of India (SEBI)

8. Reserve Bank of India (RBI)

9. The Government of India

A retail investor needs a Trading Account, Demat Account and a Bank's Savings Account to buy and sell shares of listed companies. All these three services can be provided by a single Broker, normally Banks, or you can obtain each service from a different Broker. However, it is preferable to have at least the trading and demat account with a single broker so that both are linked and available at one place.

It is important to choose your Broker carefully as the extent and quality of service offered varies from broker to broker. Therefore, choose a broker that can provide a trading platform that gives a nice trading experience, low brokerage and maintenance costs, and prompt customer support.

Depositories

There are two national depositories in India, the National Securities Depository Ltd (NSDL), and the Central Depository Services India Ltd (CDSL). NSDL commenced operations in 1996, and CDSL in 1999. Both the depositories are located in Mumbai.

One of the important roles of these depositories is to hold shares, bonds, debentures, mutual funds, etc of all investors who have invested in these instruments in electronic form.

When an investor opens a demat account with a broking firm, the broking firm decides with which depository it wants to open your account. The shares, bonds, debentures, etc that you buy are held in your account by these depositories in electronic form. When you sell any, then the depository debits it from your account.

No paper share certificates are issued nowadays. If you have inherited any paper shares, you need to get them mandatorily dematerialised before trading in them.

The depositories have made investing easy and trouble free for investors. Both depositories send monthly account statements.

Depository Participants (DPs)

A Depository Participant is one who is a member of a Depository.

Brokers are DPs and are generally members of both the depositories, but this may not be the case with all Brokers. Some prominent DPs are HDFC Securities, ICICI Securities, Zerodha, Motilal Oswal, Share Khan, etc.

Stockbrokers

Stockbrokers are Members of Stock Exchanges, but they may not be a Depository Participant. They are brokerage firms or professionals who buy and sell shares on behalf of their clients. They offer advice and portfolio management.

Banks

Banks offer the facility of opening a savings account from where you can pay for shares that you buy and receive credits for shares you sell and dividends that you receive.

Banks also offer trading platforms and one can open a Demat account as well with them.

Stock Exchanges

Simply put, a stock exchange facilitates buying and selling of stocks, derivatives and bonds of publicly listed companies.

There are two main stock exchanges in India, the Bombay Stock Exchange (BSE) and the National Stock Exchange (NSE). Both these exchanges operate out of Mumbai. However, besides the two main stock exchanges there is an exchange in Kolkata called the Calcutta Stock Exchange Ltd (CSE) which opened in 1908. At one time, there were several more regional exchanges which have now been closed down.

The Bombay Stock Exchange is the oldest exchange in Asia and the tenth largest in the world in terms of market capitalisation. It was founded in 1875 by Premchand Roychand, a prominent businessman who was popularly known as Cotton King. The exchange was recognised by the Indian Government on 31 August 1957.

The National Stock Exchange was founded in 1992, and they started operations in 1994. Today, in terms of volume alone, the National Stock

Exchange is larger than the Bombay Stock Exchange.

Both the Exchanges have the same trading mechanism, trading hours, settlement process and deal in equity, derivatives of equity, commodity and currency (including interest rate derivatives), and debt.

Commodity Exchanges

A commodity exchange deals with sale and purchase of actual commodities or derivatives. There are currently three commodity exchanges in India - Multi Commodity Exchange of India (MCX), National Commodity & Derivatives Exchange (NCDEX) and Indian Commodity Exchange Ltd (ICEX). First two are located in Mumbai, and ICEX is headquartered in Gurugram.

The MCX deals with derivatives related to bullion, base metals, energy and agricultural products whereas NCDX deals primarily in agricultural products, and ICEX in agricultural products including plantation and non-agricultural (diamond and steel).

Clearing Corporations

A Clearing Corporation is associated with a Stock Exchange and its primary objective is to oversee the handling of confirmation, settlement and delivery of transactions in the secondary markets. It is also referred to as a Clearing House or a Clearing Firm.

Securities & Exchange Board of India (SEBI)

All exchanges in India are regulated by the Securities & Exchange Board of India (SEBI). It is an autonomous body whose main aim is to protect the interests of the investors and ensure that the markets function in an orderly manner.

SEBI is headquartered in Mumbai. They also have regional offices in New Delhi, Kolkata, Chennai and Ahmedabad, and local offices in Jaipur, Kochi, Chandigarh, Guwahati, Bhubaneswar and Bengaluru and Patna.

Reserve Bank of India

There is a Central Bank in each country. In India, the Central Bank is the Reserve Bank of India (RBI), headquartered in Mumbai. In the United States it is the Federal Reserve System popularly known as Fed. In the United Kingdom it is the Bank of England. Japan's central bank is the Bank of Japan, and, in China it is People's Bank of China.

Central Banks play an important role in the monetary and banking system of a country. Briefly their role is to issue currency, regulate money supply and control different interest rates. They also control and regulate their own country's commercial banks and are the custodian of international currency. They are their government's banker, agent and advisor.

Monetary policy should not be confused with fiscal policy. Monitory policy is dictated by the RBI, whereas the fiscal policy is outlined by the executive and the government.

The Monetary Policy Committee (MPC) in India is a six-member committee chaired by the RBI Governor. It is expected to meet at least four times a year. It regulates monetary policy through various instruments at its disposal, the main ones being the Repo Rate, Reverse Repo Rate (RRR) and the Cash Reserve Ratio (CRR).

Repo Rate also called the repurchase rate is the rate at which the RBI lends money to commercial banks. Repo Rate controls inflation. When Repo Rate is increased the banks find borrowing from RBI expensive, and, when Repo Rate is decreased banks are happy to borrow.

Reverse Repo Rate (RRR) is the rate at which RBI borrows money from commercial banks. Reverse Repo Rate controls money supply. An increase in Reverse Repo Rate results in decrease in money supply, and any decrease in the rate will increase the money supply.

Cash Reserve Ratio (CRR) is the share of a commercial bank's total deposits which is required to be kept with the RBI in cash. RBI uses this to control inflation.

Any policy announcements or changes in the Repo or Reverse Repo rates or CRR affect stock markets. So, it is important to keep a watch over all these rate changes.

Stock Market Indices

To help investors understand the performance of one's investment, both stock exchanges have created several indices. These indices act as benchmarks for measuring performance of an investment. The major index on the Bombay Stock Exchange is the S&P BSE SENSEX, and NIFTY 50 on the National Stock Exchange.

The Sensex is calculated on market capitalisation weighted methodology of thirty companies selected across key sectors, whereas the Nifty 50 as the name suggests considers fifty companies in its basket. The list of these companies keeps changing based on some criteria.

Besides the two indices, SENSEX and NIFTY, both exchanges offer a whole lot of other indices based on market capitalisation, for example mid-caps or small caps; or indices based on different sectors, for example Finance, Healthcare, Information Technology, Capital Goods, Metal, Oil & Gas, etc.

Prominent World Market Indices

The prominent world market indices which one should keep an eye on are the NASDAQ-100, the S&P-500 and the DOW-30 of the United States. The United States being the most powerful economy in the world, influences all markets. All markets look up to the United States for trading cues.

The NASDAQ-100 is a basket of 100 largest and most actively traded stocks on the Nasdaq Exchange. This index includes companies across sectors except the financial ones. The S&P-500 is the Standard & Poor index comprising of nearly 500 large companies in the US, and the DOW-30 also called the Dow Jones Industrial Average Index (DJIA) comprises of 30 blue chip companies.

The important indices in Europe are the FTSE-100 of the United Kingdom, DAX-30 of Germany, and CAC-40 of France.

For markets in Asia the indices of the Shanghai Composite of China, NIKKEI-225 of Japan, STRAITS-30 of Singapore, Hang Seng of Hong Kong, Taiwan-50 of Taiwan, and KOSPI of South Korea are important.

As the sun rises from the East, Japan begins the day first followed by other Asian countries, then Europe and finally in the US, and markets open and close in this sequence. Each of the important markets take cues from the US markets.

3 BASIC RULES OF GENERAL & STOCK MARKET INVESTING

"An investment in knowledge pays the best interest"

Unknown

There are several stories where people have fallen prey to scams and lost their hard-earned money. Scamsters keep inventing new ways to trap innocent people. To protect yourself remember not to ever share your personal details with anyone, especially log-in passwords and one-time passwords (OTPs) that you receive while carrying out transactions. Promises or offers of higher or exorbitant returns should make you suspect the deal. And finally, never invest in a scheme or product that you don't understand.

Basic Rules of General Investing

There are some basic rules of investing. If you follow these rules you are sure to reap rich dividends. Most of them are very simple.

1. **Learn before you invest.** This is the most important of all rules to follow. Do not invest in a product or scheme which you do not understand.

2. **Start Investing Early.** You should commence investing early so that your investments get the time to grow. The Rule of 72 explains the relationship between time and returns. Let us say you want to double Rs 10,000 and you estimate an annual return of 12%, then time required would

be 72/12, that is 6 years. If the return is 8%, then the time required would be 72/8, that is, 9 years.

3. **Align Investments with Goals.** Investments must be goal based so that they can be monitored efficiently. Goals can be short or long term. Long term goals should be aligned with long term investments, and short-term investments to short term goals.

4. **Evaluate Risk Reward.** There is a direct relationship between risk and reward. Any investment that has the potential of generating superior returns will carry more risk. However, there is no guarantee that riskier products will deliver better returns. Hence the need to carefully evaluate risk reward. Always prepare yourself for the worst so that you are not taken by surprise and be always ready to seize opportunities when they are thrown at you.

5. **Cost Averaging.** It is very difficult to time markets, therefore, invest through systematic investment plans (SIPs) over long periods to reap benefits of cost averaging.

6. **Diversify your Portfolio.** The old saying, 'do not put all your eggs in one basket,' applies here as well. Spread your investments into various asset classes and various products in a similar asset, so that if there are losses in one, they get compensated in another.

7. **Keep Things Simple.** Choose investment plans and products that are easy to understand. Make simple financial plans which you can implement and monitor well as you go along.

8. **Be Flexible.** We all make mistakes and learning from mistakes makes one wiser. So do not fear failures. Perfection is impossible. There would always be surprises that will cause you to change your investment strategy. Periodically review your plans and be ready to make corrections.

9. **Get Rid of Emotions.** Emotions or attachments have no place in the investment world. Never get attached to a stock or an agent, dump if you do not find them useful anymore. Remember, it's all about money!

10. **Money for Meeting Emergencies.** Money that is kept aside for immediate needs or for an emergency, should be in an instrument that allows immediate access. This money can lie in your savings bank account or short-term debt mutual funds.

Basic Rules of Investing in Stock Markets

Some of the rules of general investing apply in stock market investments too. They are so important that there is no harm in repeating them.

1. **Learn Before You Invest.** This is the most important rule. Don't invest in stock markets unless you have picked up sufficient knowledge and understanding of stock markets. If you invest without understanding, then you are only a speculative investor depending on only luck to rescue you.

2. **Stay Away from Tips.** People lose their hard-earned money by buying shares of companies based on tips from family, relatives, friends, colleagues, agents or while listening to TV anchors and experts without any understanding of their own. Don't let envy drive you into entering the stock markets while you listen to people who have made money in stock markets.

3. **Invest in Companies You Understand.** Invest only in companies whose business you understand and can analyse. Companies whose products you have been using for a long time or whose products that have a great mass appeal and utility can be good choices. If you invest in good companies, the probability is that you will make good money if you remain invested in them for longer durations.

4. **Buy & Sell at the Right Price.** The price at which you buy and then subsequently sell a stock will determine your profit. Don't buy or sell your stocks in a hurry. If the price of the stock you wish is too expensive, there is nothing wrong in sitting with cash waiting for a better price.

5. **Never Hesitate to Book Losses.** You may have chosen a good company to invest in but for some reason the company's performance starts dropping and you don't foresee any recovery, then it is best to move out of that stock even if you have to book losses.

6. **Don't Time the Market.** Invest for the long term as timing the market is very difficult. Markets do best they know. Many a times you will see the markets going up and up and people keep expecting a correction, but it does not come, and many opportunities are missed. Hoping that things will

improve, is not an intelligent strategy.

7. **Diversify Your Portfolio.** Remember the old saying, 'don't put all your eggs in one basket.' it applies here too. Don't put all your money in a single stock or just one sector. No stock should have a weightage of more than 10% in the total value of your holding in stocks. Also, don't invest all your money in equity, decide on a ratio of equity to debt based on your cash requirements and risk-taking ability. When you are young, you can easily afford a higher exposure to equity, but as you get older keep reducing it because equity investments need time to grow.

8. **Don't Let Volatility Scare You.** Markets go up and go down as well. When markets are going up, everyone enjoys the phase, but markets and individual stock prices cannot keep going up all the time. Expect sometimes steep and quick falls as well as they are a normal phenomenon of stock markets. Keep your cool and don't press the panic button. Remain invested if you have chosen good companies but do worry if you have invested in wrong stocks.

9. **Keep Yourself Informed.** Stock prices move up and down for various reasons. Keep yourself well informed of matters affecting your stocks or markets in general. Markets don't like uncertainty and are quickly influenced by local, national or world events.

10. **Monitor Your Investments.** It is very important to monitor and review your investments from time to time. However, looking at them through the day is neither necessary nor desirable. Review them quarterly should be sufficient.

11. **Don't Borrow Money to Invest.** Nobody has become rich overnight. Avoid trading in stocks. Invest with small amounts but regularly over longer periods.

12. **Never Be Overconfident.** Markets have humbled many more than you may know. As retail individual investors you don't have the muscle to change the course of markets. It is easy to make money even while you buy weak stocks based on tips when markets are in a bull phase and there is a lot of liquidity in the system, and that makes many people think that they have become experts in buying and selling stocks.

As we go along, we will see how to invest our money in stock markets and reap profits while keeping all above points in mind.

4 TRADING STRATEGIES

"I will tell you how to be rich. Close the doors. Be careful when others are greedy. Be greedy when others are fearful"

Warren Buffett

There are basically two types of shares. However, in this book we will discuss listed equity shares only.

1. **Equity Shares.** These are the most common type of shares that are traded on stock exchanges. Every share has a face value. Shareholders receive dividends when companies declare them and have voting rights.

2. **Preference Shares.** There are several types of preference shares. As the name suggests these are issued on preferential terms. If a company goes into liquidation, preferential shareholders get preference over equity shareholders when pay outs happen. These shareholders do not enjoy any voting rights.

Investing Strategies

There are two ways of investing in stock markets by adopting a:

1. Passive Strategy, or an

2. Active Strategy

Active investing is more expensive as it involves a greater turnover of stocks compared to passive investing. Passive investing is less expensive and also more tax efficient.

Passive & Indexed Strategies

Passive investing is simply buying and holding strategy. The passive investor buys shares or indices and holds them for longer durations in the hope of harvesting greater gains and reducing chances of losses. This type of investing is more suitable for retail investors, and it is this strategy that we shall be focussing on in this book.

Active Trading Strategies

Under an active strategy an investor aims to make profits from short term fluctuations in stock prices. Such a strategy requires a high level of skill, is risky and best left to professionals. Active traders make buy and sell decisions very quickly and depend on short term trends, rather than on fundamentals of a company. There are essentially four types of active strategies traders employ:

1. **Day Trading.** In this strategy, as the name suggests, shares are bought and sold on the same day. No overnight positions are held. The trader depends on reading the daily trend charts.

2. **Position Trading.** In this strategy shares are bought and held over longer periods, sometimes over a few weeks or even months. Position trading use longer term charts to study trends to decide on when to buy and sell.

3. **Swing Trading.** Swing traders take advantage of change in price trends, either upwards or downwards. These trades are generally held for more than a day. These are complicated trades involving algorithms that signal buying and selling.

4. **Scalping.** These are very short-term strategies that exploit gaps in bid-ask spreads and order flows. Such strategies work best when markets are silent and not prone to large market fluctuations.

Active trading strategies require significant investment in hardware and software, special training and skill sets. These are, therefore, for professional traders. However, these days novices have also jumped into this, nearly all of them end up losing money.

You will understand more about these strategies after you go through the chapters on Technical Analysis in Segment III of this book.

Stock Derivatives

Derivatives are contracts that derive a value from underlying assets and securities. In case of stock derivatives, the underlying asset is a stock. Derivatives are used for risk management.

Derivative is basically a contract between two parties, the hedger and the speculator or trader. Hedgers in this case are the stock owners who wish to transfer future price fluctuation. The speculator or trader is the risk taker.

Why traders take this risk? Traders take this risk because they have an opportunity to take positions on larger volumes of shares at cheaper transaction costs as no transfer of shares is involved.

Trading in Stock Derivatives

Derivative trading products are:

1. **Forwards.** These contracts are signed between two parties to buy or sell shares on any future date on a price agreed upon at the time of signing the contract. These contracts are customised as per requirements of the two parties. These contracts are not traded through stock exchanges but over the counter, normally by financial institutions.

2. **Futures.** Futures are traded through the stock exchanges. These are standardised forward contracts. You can buy or sell these contracts during or at the time of expiry of these contracts. These contracts expose you to huge gains or huge losses.

3. **Options.** Options give you the right to buy or sell shares for an agreed upon price within a specified time period. This works well when traders aspire for huge gains but limited losses. There is a premium charged for buying option contracts. Options are of two types, call option and put

option. Call option gives the buyer the right to buy shares, and the put option the right to sell shares.

Contracts that have an expiry period, treat the last Thursday of the month as the expiry date. If that day happens to be a holiday, then the previous day is considered as expiry day.

A stock derivative comprises shares of a particular company in fixed lots. The number of shares in a lot is decided by the stock exchange and varies from company to company.

Understanding how Futures Work

Let us understand with an example the working of a derivative trade in futures.

Suppose you buy a single futures contract of a company XYZ consisting of 50 shares on a particular day when it's share is trading at say Rs 1,000 per share. This means that you are willing to buy or sell the share at Rs 1,000 on the expiry date. However, you can decide to sell before the expiry date or on the expiry day.

Let us further assume that the day you sell, the price is Rs 1,100 per share, your gain would be Rs 100 per share, and the total gains would be Rs (100x50), that is, Rs 5,000. However, if the price on the day you decide to sell, falls to Rs 950 per share, your loss would be Rs 50 per share and the total loss would be Rs (50x50), that is, Rs 2,500.

Payoffs & Charges for Futures Contracts

The main payoffs for traders in futures are margin payments. You cannot buy or sell without margins. There are different types of margins and these are decided by stock exchanges as a percentage of total value of a derivative contract. The different margins are:

1. **Initial Margin.** Initial margin is defined as a percentage of your open positions and is set for different positions by exchanges. These amounts fluctuate on a daily basis depending on market value of your open position.

2. **Exposure Margin.** Exposure margin is levied on the total value of the

contract that you buy or sell. This margin is set by exchanges to control volatility and excessive speculation.

3. **Mark to Market Margin.** This margin covers the difference between the cost of contract and its closing price on the day the contract is purchased. After the day the contract is purchased, this margin is recalculated each day based on the difference of purchase price and closing price.

4. **Premium Margin.** This margin is paid to the seller when you buy a contract. It is usually paid on a per share basis. If you sell a contract, then you will receive this margin money.

Margin payments help traders dealing in derivatives to make gains by making small payments instead of paying full value of contracts.

Apart from margins, you also have to pay other charges like transaction charges, stamp duty, GST, securities transaction tax (STT) and SEBI tax.

Trading in futures is complex. You should not get into it unless you understand it fully.

Understanding how Options Work

Suppose you hold shares of a company XYZ and the current price of each shares is Rs 100. You expect the price to go down, so you enter into an options contract to sell your shares at Rs 97 per share and pay a premium of Rs 2 to the buyer.

Assuming, the market falls as anticipated, and the share price drops to Rs 90. In this case you still have the option of selling it at Rs 97 saving yourself a further loss if you had to sell it at Rs 90.

Consider the other case when the market goes up, and the share price moves to say Rs 110. In this case you can choose not to exercise your option to sell and go ahead with the sale of shares at Rs 110 by paying a premium of Rs 2.

Options are traded as call or put options.

Understanding how Call Options Work

Call option gives the buyer the option to buy shares. Let us understand with an example how call options work.

Let us say a stock XYZ is trading at Rs 257 on a particular day, and a trader enters into a call option contract to buy the share at Rs 260 with a premium of Rs 1. Now the buyer has a right to buy the share at Rs 260 any time before the contract expiry date even if the share price moves to say Rs 280 or beyond.

Understanding how Put Options Work

Put option gives the seller the option to sell. An example of this would be as explained below.

Let us say the stock XYZ is trading at Rs 257 on a particular day, and a trader enters into a put option contract at an exercise price of Rs 250 per share with a premium of Rs 2. Assume the price of the share drops to Rs 230 by the end of expiry date. The seller in this case can sell his shares at Rs 250 thus earning a profit of Rs (250-230-2), that is, Rs 18 per share.

You would have noticed that trading in options is also complex. You should get into this also only if you really understand it well.

My personal advice to retail investors is to adopt the passive investing strategy only and stay away from trading in stocks.

5 ANALYSING: ECONOMY & INDUSTRY

"Buy when everyone else is selling and hold when everyone is buying. This is not merely a catchy slogan. It is the very essence of successful investments"

J Paul Getty

Wealth is created only by making intelligent long-term investments through fundamentally strong companies. Fundamental analysis helps us in identifying fundamentally strong companies. You do not need any special finance background for carrying out fundamental analysis which you will realise after reading this chapter. All that you need is freely available data and an analytical mind.

Fundamental analysis has three stages:

1. Economy Analysis

2. Industry Analysis

3. Company Analysis

If we start analysing the economy first and then analyse the industry and the company, such a process is called a Top to Bottom Approach. Alternately, if we begin with company analysis and thereafter industry and economy, then it is called a Bottom to Top Approach. Either of the approaches are fine, you can choose any, but I personally prefer the Top to Bottom Approach as it helps you to firstly identify strong sectors in the economy from which you can pick the strongest stocks to invest in.

ECONOMY ANALYSIS

The financial health of a nation can be understood by analysing its economy as it helps us to identify threats and opportunities that may affect the company's performance. However, analysing a country's economy is not easy, as it requires special skills, but we can analyse some of the parameters that will help us to conclude whether the economy is doing well or not:

1. **Gross Domestic Product (GDP).** GDP of a nation is an estimate of the total goods and services produced by it during a specific period, which may be quarterly or annual. It is an important statistic that indicates whether the economy is growing or contracting by comparing it to previous figures. GDP is calculated either by adding up all the money spent by consumers, businesses and the government or by adding all the money received by all participants in the economy. Such a figure would be called Nominal GDP and after being corrected for inflation will be called Real GDP. Higher the GDP, better is the economy.

2. **Inflation.** Inflation indicates decline in purchasing power of a given currency over time. Most commonly used inflation indices are Wholesale Price Index (WPI) or Consumer Price Index (CPI). WPI measures and tracks the changes in the price of goods in the stages before the retail level whereas CPI measures and tracks the weighted average prices of goods and services used primarily by consumers. Inflation can be good and bad depending on which side you are. Inflation is bad when it is too high or too low, but a steady rate is desirable. Inflation is controlled by the Reserve Bank of India (RBI) through its fiscal policy

3. **Foreign Exchange Reserve.** These are assets held as reserves by RBI in foreign currencies. These many include foreign currencies, bonds, treasury bills or other government securities. Most of these reserves are held as US dollars in India. These assets serve many purposes including controlling exchange rates and as back up if local currency rapidly devalues and becomes insolvent. A healthy and growing reserve is good for the economy.

4. **Balance of Payments (BOP).** Balance of Payment is a statement of all transactions made by entities of one country with the rest of the world over a period of time, usually over a quarter or a year. If our total exports are more than the imports, then we have a surplus balance of payment which is healthy. On the contrary, if the imports are more than the exports, then we are deficient balance of payment. the deficiency is then met from the reserves which is not good. Our biggest expense is on the import bills of oil and gold.

5. **Growth of Industries.** Identify industries that are growing at a higher pace than others. Such an indication can come from yearly budget announcements, government policies and by studying stock indices and ETFs.

6. **Interest Rates.** Interest rates are regulated by the Reserve Bank of India. Lower the interest rates, better for the corporates as borrowing becomes cheaper.

7. **Tax Structure.** A steady and friendly taxation policy benefits investors and corporates.

8. **Monsoon.** Almost 16% of India's GDP comes from the agriculture sector. This sector employs nearly 50% of the nation's work force. In India, agricultural output is still dependant on a good monsoon. Keep this in mind.

9. **Political Stability.** Political instability is not desirable as it is detrimental to a country's growth.

Understanding and analysing the above factors are sufficient for us to conclude whether the economy is doing well or not, and which sectors in the economy are doing better than others. As many businesses are spread across several countries, the economic conditions prevailing in those countries should also be assessed as it will affect business profitability.

Having analysed the economy and identified potentially strong sectors we move to analysing the selected sectors.

INDUSTRY ANALYSIS

For an investor, industry analysis is a means to help understand a company's position relative to other participants in the industry, and in identifying opportunities and threats so as to get an idea of the present as well as future.

An industry is defined as a group of companies offering similar products and/or services. Therefore, while analysing a company within an industry, see that you choose the right sub-group or sector. For example, a chemical industry has several sub sectors or groups like dyes, paints, pharmaceuticals, fertilisers, varnishes, etc.

Demand and supply are the primary factors of any market. Understanding the present and predicting the future demand and supply position gives an indication of the growth probability of the sector as well as the company under consideration.

Porter's famous 5 Forces model also known as Competitive Forces Model is widely used for industry analysis:

1. **Intensity of Industry Rivalry.** The number of market participants and the market share of each of them along with exit costs related to fixed assets, government restrictions, labour unions, etc make the participants fight harder.

2. **Threat of Potential New Entrants.** If a firm can enter easily into the same industry sector, then the companies in the sector will face constant threat of losing their market share. On the other hand, if entry is difficult then the company will enjoy competitive advantage for long.

3. **Bargaining Power of Suppliers.** If the industry has a small number of suppliers, they will enjoy considerable bargaining power and it may affect the company's product price and quality.

4. **Bargaining Power of Buyers.** If there are more companies within an industry and there is a single or few buyers or consumers who buy the bulk of production, then the consumer will enjoy bargaining power, thus negotiating lower prices.

5. **Threat of Substitute Goods/Services.** Competitors will always endeavour to offer a cheaper or better quality of goods/services and bring down profitability of another company.

The answer to all above questions, will lead you to a clear understanding of the growth potential of the industry sector as well as the company you wish to analyse.

6 WHAT TO READ IN ANNUAL REPORTS OF COMPANIES

"Only those who are asleep make no mistakes"

Ingvar Kamprad

All listed companies are required to publish mandatorily two reports: a Quarterly Report for each quarter of a financial year within 45 days after the end of each quarter, and an Annual Report for each financial year within 60 days after the end of every financial year.

If a company fails to adhere to above timelines, it may be assumed that there is something terribly wrong with the company.

Quarterly and annual reports are mandatorily required to be published by every listed company and made available to its shareholders and are posted on their website for potential shareholders. All information published in these reports is official and any misrepresentation is a legal offence.

As the names suggest, quarterly and annual reports contain details of the company's quarterly and annual performance while comparing them to previous quarters or years. Although quarterly and annual reports contain all the financial statements, the annual reports are much more exhaustive than quarterly reports, and therefore, annual reports are used for carrying out fundamental analysis. You must read through the annual reports of a company before making any investing decisions.

There is no fixed format for writing an annual report. No two reports are similar. However, all annual reports must contain all information as stipulated by SEBI.

Annual reports are lengthy and run into several pages and have a huge amount of data. The report helps in understanding the company and the sector in which it operates. Important contents of an annual report that must be read:

1. **Company Profile.** In the company profile you will find details with regard to promoters, directors, auditors, bankers, company secretary, company's vision, some financial highlights, company's products and its history, etc.

2. **Notice of Annual General Meeting.** This may or may not be attached to the annual report and its importance lies in the details it provides of any resolutions that are required to be passed.

3. **Chairman's Message.** This is important as it gives an overview of the company's performance and plans going ahead.

4. **Report from Directors.** In addition to the Chairman's message, there may be reports from individual directors.

5. **Management's Discussions & Analysis.** This is a very important part of the report. Here the management gives an overview of the industry or sector in which the company is operating, highlighting the past and future growth of the sector and the company along with associated risks the sector and the company may face in the future.

6. **Shareholding Pattern.** Here you can know who all are invested in the company.

7. **Auditor's Report.** Look for serious breaches that may have been pointed out by auditors.

8. **Financial Statements.** Profit & Loss Statement, Balance Sheet and Cash Flow Statement are contained in the financial statements. Detailed explanations of line items are given in the Notes. You should analyse the consolidated statements instead of the stand-alone ones.

9. **Schedules & Notes to the Accounts.** These provide more details and explanations of the financial statements.

10. **Corporate Governance Report.** This part of the report tells us how well the company is following laid down rules and regulations.

After reading the annual report you should be able to draw inferences and conclusions that are positive or negative for the company.

7 QUALITATIVE ANALYSIS OF A COMPANY

"The key to making money in stock markets not to get scared out of them"

Peter Lynch

For analysing a company, you have to study its annual reports, and the analysis is required to be done in two parts:

1. Qualitative Analysis, and

2. Quantitative Analysis.

Qualitative Analysis

Qualitative analysis deals with non-numeric aspects of a company, and since these are non-numeric, they are difficult to analyse. For retail investors, gathering data for qualitative analysis is difficult as they have no access to managements, and they have to sift information through company's annual report, news reports, company's web site, listening to quarterly earnings conference call extracts, broker reports, etc.

The aim of carrying out such an analysis should be to find answers to questions listed below so that you can assess the risks involved while investing in a business and you can take an informed decision:

1. **Company's Core Business & History.** How is the company earning money? What is its history?

2. **Company's Geographic Exposure & its Customers.** Which geographies the company's business is exposed to? How many big or dedicated customers it has? Does the company serve only businesses or end users also? What segment of customers are served? Are they serving only urban areas or rural areas as well?

3. **Management Quality.** What is the background of the management team? Is the management adequately experienced to handle the business? Do they score high on honesty and integrity? Is the management motivated and having a growth mindset? Do they have business transactions with their relatives? Are their salaries reasonable? Is there any political affiliation? What percentage of shares have been pledged by the promoters?

4. **Company Organisation.** Does the company have a suitable organisational structure? Is there a succession plan in place?

5. **Competitive Advantage.** Is the company enjoying any competitive advantage over its peers? What are the advantages?

6. **Corporate Governance.** Is the company legally complying to government's policies? Is the company treating all its stakeholders fairly? Are company's rules well aligned with the company's mission and vision?

7. **Market Share.** What is the company's market share?

8. **Regulatory Constraints.** What are the regulatory constraints under which the business is to be carried out? Is the company adhering to these regulations?

Above aspects may not be easy to uncover as they are subtle in nature. However, a well-informed investor can easily figure this out by studying the company's annual report or through news reports.

8 QUANTITATIVE ANALYSIS: FINANCIAL STATEMENTS

"If stock market experts were so expert, they would be buying stocks, not selling advice

Norman Ralph Augustine

Quantitative analysis deals with numeric financial numbers. The results of this analysis should provide an insight into the intrinsic value of a stock. Intrinsic value of a stock is the anticipated or calculated value of a stock determined through the process of fundamental analysis. It is this price a rational investor should be ready to pay.

Quantitative analysis is done by analysing the following financial statements:

1. Profit & Loss Statement (also called the P&L Statement),

2. Balance Sheet, and

3. Cash Flow Statement.

Understanding company's financial statements is very important for an investor, especially for investors in stock markets. Financial statements reveal the health of a company. Study of these provide you with a tool for such assessment.

Financial statements can be accessed from the websites of individual companies, stock exchanges, money control, value research, etc.

Financial statements could be quarterly or annual. These reports could be STANDALONE FINANCIAL REPORTS or CONSOLIDATED FINANCIAL REPORTS. Standalone reports reflect data related to the company's head office plus its branches in India or abroad whereas consolidated reports include data of the standalone report plus of any SUBSIDIARIES, ASSOCIATES and JOINT VENTURES. Therefore, it is better to analyse consolidated reports.

A company in which the parent company (also called the holding company) holds more than 50% of its shares or has more than 20% weightage in its decision making is called its SUBSIDIARY. If the parent company holds 100% of the subsidiary company's shares, then that subsidiary is called a wholly owned subsidiary.

A company in which the parent company holds more than 20% but less than 50% of its shares is called its ASSOCIATE.

As per accounting standards, if the parent company holds less than 20% shares in a company, it may not reflect its data in the consolidated financial statements.

A company may join hands with another company for purposes of completing a specific project. Such an arrangement is called a JOINT VENTURE.

While analysing financial statements it would be prudent to consider statements of three to five years to give a complete sense of the company's performance.

UNDERSTANDING PROFIT & LOSS STATEMENT

Profit & Loss statements are also called Income Statements or P&L Statements. These statements cover a period of one financial year only and consist of three parts:

1. **Revenue.** Revenue is nothing else but the company's income from its normal operations after excluding discounts and returns. Gross revenue or Net Revenue, also called the TOP LINE, is sum total of incomes from main operations, other incomes that are incidental to the business and other

incomes from non-operational sources.

2. **Expenses.** Expenses are costs that a company incurs to generate income. A company incurs two type of expenses, CAPITAL & REVENUE. Capital expenses are those that are against creation of assets like machinery, buildings, furniture, etc and are accounted in the Balance Sheet and not in the P&L statement. On the other hand, Revenue Expenses are made to meet operational costs like salaries, maintenance and upkeep, rents, research and development, etc and are considered in the P&L statement. Capital expenses are also called CAPEX and Revenue expenses as Operating Expenses (OPEX).

3. **Profit or Loss.** If Revenue is more than expenses, then there is profit for the company. If the Revenue is less than Expenses, then the company has made a loss. This is also the net income that has accrued to the company and is called the BOTTOM LINE.

Statement of Profit and Loss
for the year ended 31st March 2020

			(Rs. in Crores)
		Note No.	2019-20	2018-19
I)	INCOME:			
	Revenue from operations	26	9,856.66	10,588.31
	Other income	27	63.94	38.50
	Total income (I)		**9,920.60**	**10,626.81**
II)	EXPENSES:			
	Cost of materials consumed	28	6,519.80	6,988.58
	Purchase of stock-in-trade		6.17	18.51
	Changes in inventories of finished goods, work-in-progress and stock-in-trade	29	(259.58)	(36.85)
	Employee benefit expenses	30	666.40	637.66
	Other expenses	33	1,558.89	1,569.07
	Total Expenses (II)		**8,491.68**	**9,176.97**
III)	**EARNINGS BEFORE INTEREST, TAX, DEPRECIATION AND AMORTISATION EXPENSES (I-II)**		**1,428.92**	**1,449.84**
	Finance costs	31	9.40	6.05
	Depreciation and amortisation expenses	32	362.63	313.50
IV)	**INTEREST, DEPRECIATION AND AMORTISATION EXPENSES**		**372.03**	**319.55**
V)	**PROFIT BEFORE EXCEPTIONAL ITEMS AND TAX (III-IV)**		**1,056.89**	**1,130.29**
VI)	**EXCEPTIONAL ITEMS**	46	(21.70)	108.29
VII)	**PROFIT BEFORE TAX (V+VI)**		**1,035.19**	**1,238.58**
VIII)	**TAX EXPENSES:**	21		
	1. Current tax [net of provision for earlier years Rs. 2.86 crs (PY: net of reversal of provision for earlier years Rs. 3.11 crs)]		280.92	358.42
	2. Deferred tax		(71.24)	36.11
			209.68	**394.53**
IX)	**PROFIT FOR THE YEAR (VII-VIII)**		**825.51**	**844.05**
X)	**OTHER COMPREHENSIVE INCOME (OCI)**			
	Other comprehensive Income not to be reclassified subsequently to profit or loss:			
	a) Re-measurement gains/(losses) on defined benefit plans	36	(11.16)	2.94
	Income tax effect		2.81	(1.02)
	b) Net (loss)/ gain on investment in equity shares / units accounted at fair value		(11.47)	(3.82)
	Income tax effect		2.04	1.47
	Other Comprehensive Income for the year		**(17.78)**	**(0.43)**
XI)	**TOTAL COMPREHENSIVE INCOME FOR THE YEAR (IX+X)**		**807.73**	**843.62**
	Earnings per share - Basic and Diluted (Nominal value Re. 1 per share (PY Re. 1 per share)]	34	9.71	9.93
	Significant accounting policies	1		

The above is an actual P&L Statement of Exide Industries. Let us see the meaning and significance of each line item.

The first thing to notice is that this Statement of Profit & Loss is for the year ended 31 Mar 2020, that is for the financial year 2019-20, and all currency values are expressed in rupees and in crores.

In an income statement of an annual report, there are always at least two columns that show all data for two consecutive periods. This helps in understanding a company's performance over two years. In this case, the figures for financial year 2018-19 are given for comparison.

There is also a column called Notes. Detailed explanation of each line item can be seen while referring to the relevant note mentioned against it.

Investors use the Income Statement to check for quantum of profits a company is making as well as Earnings per Share (EPS). Therefore, the Top and Bottom Lines are of interest to investors.

Income

The first line item is Income under which you have three lines, revenue from operations, other income and total income. The revenue from operations is explained in Note 26 and other income in Note 27.

26 REVENUE FROM OPERATIONS

		(Rs. in Crores)
	2019-20	2018-19
Sale of products	9,809.00	10,564.89
Other operating income		
Export incentive	33.75	8.46
Scrap sales	4.44	6.42
Income from service / installation	9.47	8.54
	9,856.66	**10,588.31**

27 OTHER INCOME

		(Rs. in Crores)
	2019-20	2018-19
Interest income on :		
Income tax refunds	4.79	2.10
Financial assets carried at amortised cost	0.94	0.71
Dividend income on		
Long term Investments in subsidiaries	17.04	6.85
Current investments in mutual funds designated at FVTPL	20.11	11.01
Other non-operating income		
Gain on fair value of investments in mutual funds units designated at FVTPL	0.42	0.48
Net foreign exchange gain	11.88	9.13
Rental income from investment property	2.12	-
Others	6.64	7.22
	63.94	**38.50**

On studying Note 26, we understand that the Revenue from Operations came from the Sale of Products amounting to Rs 9,809 crores and other operating income consisting of Rs 33.75 crores from Export Incentive, Rs 4.44 crores from Scrap Sales and Rs 9.47 crores from service/installation.

Note 27 explains the details of Other Income which are quite self-explanatory. What is notable is that this income is not because of the company's primary activities.

It is important to note that the total income for the financial year 2019-20 is Rs 9920.60 crores which is less than the total income of the previous financial year 2018-19, more particularly the income from operations.

Expenses

The next part of the P&L Statement relates to the Rs 8,491.68 crores of Expenses the company has made during the year.

II) EXPENSES:			
Cost of materials consumed	28	6,519.80	6,988.58
Purchase of stock-in-trade		6.17	18.51
Changes in inventories of finished goods, work-in-progress and stock-in-trade	29	(259.58)	(36.85)
Employee benefit expenses	30	666.40	637.66
Other expenses	33	1,558.89	1,569.07
Total Expenses (II)		**8,491.68**	**9,176.97**

The details of expenses incurred against cost of materials consumed can be understood from Note 28.

28 COST OF MATERIALS CONSUMED

		(Rs. in Crores)
	2019-20	2018-19
Opening stock	451.64	454.82
Add: Purchases	6,645.56	6,985.40
	7,097.20	**7,440.22**
Less: Closing stock	577.40	451.64
	6,519.80	**6,988.58**

Opening stock of Rs 451.64 is the cost that was not consumed in the previous year and is accounted for in this year which is equivalent to the closing stock shown in 2018-19. The purchases made during the year are of Rs 6,645.56 which is less than the purchases made in the previous year.

The stock that is not consumed is shown against Closing Stock and this amount of Rs 577.40 crores is rightly reduced and total cost of materials consumed is shown as Rs 6,519.80 crores.

Purchase of Stock in Trade is shown as Rs 6.17 crores. Stock in Trade relates to finished goods the company has purchased to carry on its business.

The next item line is changes in inventories of finished goods, work in progress and stock in trade.

Change in inventory of finished goods refers to cost of manufacturing that was incurred in the past, but the finished product was sold during the current year.

Let us see the details in Note 29.

29 CHANGES IN INVENTORIES OF FINISHED GOODS, WORK-IN-PROGRESS AND STOCK-IN-TRADE

(Rs. in Crores)

	2019-20	2018-19
Opening Stock		
Work-in-progress	530.04	466.60
Finished goods	773.68	792.96
Stock-in-trade	5.24	12.55
	1,308.96	**1,272.11**

	2019-20	2018-19
Closing Stock		
Work-in-progress	707.76	530.04
Finished goods	854.28	773.68
Stock-in-trade	6.50	5.24
	1,568.54	**1,308.96**
Net increase in inventories of finished goods, work-in-progress and stock-in-trade	(259.58)	(36.85)

The details shown under opening stock refers to the previous year's carry forward, and the details under closing stock refer to the current year. The opening stock less the closing stock gives the net increase in inventories of finished goods, work in progress and stock in trade of Rs (259.58) crores. The breakdown of this amount can be worked out as under:

1. Work in progress = (530.04-707.76) = Rs (177.72) crores. These refer to goods that are yet to be finished and not available for sale.

2. Finished goods = (773.68-854.28) = Rs (80.60) crores. These are finished goods, ready for sale but could not be sold.

3. Stock in trade = (5.24-6.50) = Rs (1.26) crores. These are finished goods that the company purchased but could not use.

The next line item is employee benefit expenses of Rs 666.40 crores which refer to salaries and other benefits paid by the company. Details of this expense can be seen in Note 30 which is self-explanatory.

30 EMPLOYEE BENEFIT EXPENSES

	(Rs. in Crores)	
	2019-20	2018-19
Salaries, wages and bonus	567.83	533.93
Contribution to provident and other funds (Refer Note 36)	34.08	32.80
Staff welfare expenses	64.49	70.93
	666.40	**637.66**

Finally, other expenses are shown as Rs 1,558.89 crores and their details are given in Note 33. The list is long but again self-explanatory.

33 OTHER EXPENSES

	(Rs. in Crores)	
	2019-20	2018-19
Stores and spare parts consumed	68.24	83.71
Power and fuel	331.59	332.57
Battery charging / battery assembly expenses	92.75	106.68
Repairs and maintenance		
Buildings	7.17	9.62
Plant & machinery	25.11	31.59
Others	2.16	2.00
Software expenses	39.65	12.99
Rent & hire charges	41.00	38.66
Rates and taxes	9.12	6.42
Insurance	8.56	9.30
Commission	1.13	3.88
Royalty and technical aid fees	53.37	53.21
Warranty expenses	269.64	261.98
Publicity and sales promotion	68.01	78.45
Freight & forwarding (net)	276.63	294.58
After sales services	68.11	67.09
Clearing and forwarding expenses	36.06	34.55
Travelling & conveyance	33.61	42.44
Bank charges	1.67	1.43
Communication costs	4.25	4.86
Donations	0.02	0.06
Directors' sitting fees	0.24	0.24
Loss on property, plant and equipment sold/discarded (net)	2.07	0.34
Auditors' remuneration:		
As Auditors *		
- For Statutory audit	0.49	0.49
- For Limited reviews	0.39	0.30
- For Others	0.05	0.05
As Tax auditors	0.07	0.07
Other services	0.09	0.02
Out of pocket expenses	0.10	0.09
Miscellaneous expenses (refer Note 33.1)	117.54	91.40
	1,558.89	**1,569.07**

So, we see that when we add up all expenses, we get the total expenses incurred by the company as Rs 8,491.58 crores.

The next item on the P&L Statement is the Earnings Before Interest, Tax, Depreciation and Amortisation Expenses.

Depreciation and Amortisation Expenses are obtained by subtracting the total expenses from total income, that is Rs (9920.60-8491.68) = Rs 1428.92 crores.

III)	EARNINGS BEFORE INTEREST, TAX, DEPRECIATION AND AMORTISATION EXPENSES (I-II)		1,428.92	1,449.84
	Finance costs	31	9.40	6.05
	Depreciation and amortisation expenses	32	362.63	313.50
IV)	INTEREST, DEPRECIATION AND AMORTISATION EXPENSES		372.03	319.55
V)	PROFIT BEFORE EXCEPTIONAL ITEMS AND TAX (III-IV)		1,056.89	1,130.29
VI)	EXCEPTIONAL ITEMS	46	(21.70)	108.29
VII)	PROFIT BEFORE TAX (V+VI)		1,035.19	1,238.58
VIII)	TAX EXPENSES:	21		
	1. Current tax [net of provision for earlier years Rs. 2.86 crs (PY: net of reversal of provision for earlier years Rs. 3.11 crs)]		280.92	358.42
	2. Deferred tax		(71.24)	36.11
			209.68	394.53
IX)	PROFIT FOR THE YEAR (VII-VIII)		825.51	844.05
X)	OTHER COMPREHENSIVE INCOME (OCI)			
	Other comprehensive income not to be reclassified subsequently to profit or loss:			
	a) Re-measurement gains/(losses) on defined benefit plans	36	(11.16)	2.94
	Income tax effect		2.81	(1.02)
	b) Net (loss)/ gain on investment in equity shares / units accounted at fair value		(11.47)	(3.82)
	Income tax effect		2.04	1.47
	Other Comprehensive Income for the year		**(17.78)**	**(0.43)**

The finance cost is an expense that refers to the interest paid by the company from whom they have borrowed money. This amount is Rs 9.40 crores. Details of this are shown in Note 31.

31 FINANCE COSTS

	2019-20	2018-19
		(Rs. in Crores)
Interest expenses	6.95	6.05
Interest on lease liabilities	2.45	-
	9.40	**6.05**

Depreciation and amortisation are another expenses. Depreciation refers to reduced value of all tangible assets over time, and amortisation refers to reduced value of intangible assets over time. Tangible assets can be plant and machinery, buildings, etc. Intangible assets are brand value, copyrights, etc. The company has incurred a cost of Rs 362.63 crores details of which are available in Note 32.

32 DEPRECIATION AND AMORTISATION

	2019-20	2018-19
		(Rs. in Crores)
Depreciation of property, plant and equipment	350.60	305.13
Amortisation of intangible assets	10.54	8.37
Depreciation of investment property	0.35	-
Depreciation of right-of-use asset	1.14	-
	362.63	**313.50**

The expense shown against depreciation of tangible assets like property, plant and equipment is Rs 350.60 crores, amortisation expense is Rs 10.54 crores, depreciation of investment property is Rs 0.35 crores, and Rs 1.14 crores is expense towards depreciation of right of use asset. A right of use asset is an asset that the company has the right to use a leased property for its use. Total expense towards depreciation and amortisation is Rs 362.63

crores.

Next line item is interest, depreciation and amortisation expenses of Rs 370.02 crores which is total of depreciation, amortisation and finance expenses.

Profit before exceptional items and tax is shown as Rs 1,056.89 crores. This is obtained by subtracting total expense of depreciation, amortisation and finance from earnings before interest, tax, depreciation and amortisation, that is (1,428.92-372.63) = Rs 1,056.89 crores.

Expense towards exceptional items is Rs (21.07) crores and details are shown in Note 46. Exceptional expenses are onetime expenses.

46 Exceptional Item for current year represents the duty/tax paid under the Sabka Vishwas - (Legacy Dispute Resolution) Scheme, 2019 and for previous year represents profit on sale of property at Guindy, Tamil Nadu.

Here, the company has received Rs 21.07 crores that was paid earlier, hence shown as negative.

Profit before tax, therefore, works out by adding the amount received under exceptional items to the profit before exceptional items, that is [1,056.89+(21.07)] = Rs 1,035.19 crores.

Tax expenses are shown as Rs 209.68 crores that includes current tax of Rs 280.92 crores, and Rs (71.24) crores as deferred tax. Current tax is the corporate tax that the company has paid or will pay during the year, and tax that is postponed is called deferred tax. Since the figure against deferred tax is negative, it means that the company has received some relief from the earlier projected amount against deferred tax.

Profit for the Year

Profit for the year is obtained by subtracting tax expenses from profit before tax, that is (1,035.19-209.68) = Rs 825.51 crores which is less than the previous year's profit of Rs 844.05 crores.

Other Comprehensive Income

Other comprehensive income refers to revenues, expenses, gains and losses that are yet to be realised and are excluded from the net income in a

P&L Statement. A sum of Rs (17.78) crores is shown against this.

Total comprehensive income for the year is obtained by adding the other comprehensive income from the profit for the year, that is [844.05 +(17.78)] = Rs 807.73 crores which is less than Rs 843.62 of previous year.

Earnings Per Share

Finally, the line which relates to earning per share and all calculation details are given in Note 34.

34   EARNINGS PER SHARE (EPS)

	2019-20	2018-19
Details for calculation of basic and diluted earning per share		
Profit after tax as per Statement of Profit and Loss (Rs. in Crores)	825.51	844.05
Weighted average number of equity share (Numbers)	85,00,00,000	85,00,00,000
Basic and diluted earning per share (Rs.)	9.71	9.93

You will notice that profit after tax has been taken for calculating EPS and not total comprehensive income because comprehensive income is yet to be realised.

The EPS for the current year is Rs 9.71 which is less than Rs 9.93 of previous year.

The P&L Statement must be read in conjunction with the Balance Sheet and the Cash Flow Statement as they are all connected with each other.

UNDERSTANDING BALANCE SHEETS

A P&L statement shows details of profit and loss, the balance sheet consists of details relating to assets and liabilities. Balance Sheet shows the position of assets and liabilities as on the end date of a financial year unlike the P&L account that shows data for only one financial year.

ASSETS are anything that the company owns and that which provide any future economic benefit. Assets increase the equity value of a company and are classified as:

1. **Current Assets.** These assets are short term assets that can be liquidated into cash within twelve months. These assets include cash, trade receivables, inventories, short term investments, etc.

2. **Non-current Assets.** Assets that take more than twelve months to convert into cash are called non-current assets. These assets can be land, building, machinery, long term investments, intangible assets like patents, copyrights, etc.

The sum of current and non-current assets are the total assets of a company. LIABILITIES are anything that a company owes to others. Similar to assets, liabilities are also classified as:

1. **Current Liabilities.** These liabilities are short term that are required to be paid in the next twelve months. These liabilities include payments towards employees, taxes, short term debts, etc.

2. **Non-current Liabilities.** Liabilities that are required to be paid after twelve months are called non-current liabilities. These can be long term debts, trade payables, differed tax payments, etc.

Balance Sheet
as at 31st March 2020

(Rs. in Crores)

		Note No.	March 31, 2020	March 31, 2019
i) ASSETS				
1) Non-Current Assets				
a)	Property, plant and equipment	2(a)	2,275.48	2,265.97
b)	Capital work-in-progress	2(a)	296.88	254.93
c)	Investment property	2(b)	34.23	-
d)	Right-of-use asset	2(c)	27.44	-
e)	Intangible assets	3	36.47	31.30
f)	Financial assets			
(i)	Investments	4	2,052.07	1,945.48
(ii)	Trade receivables	5	0.10	0.18
(iii)	Loans	6	17.19	18.18
g)	Current tax assets (net)		64.72	88.62
h)	Other non-current assets	7	98.00	95.79
			4,902.58	**4,700.45**
2) Current Assets				
a)	Inventories	8	2,192.27	1,803.97
b)	Financial assets			
(i)	Investments	9	18.73	253.91
(ii)	Trade receivables	10	815.30	1,081.04
(iii)	Cash and cash equivalents	11	144.87	64.70
(iv)	Bank balances other than (iii) above	12	9.72	8.85
(v)	Loans	13	14.98	13.98
(vi)	Other financial assets	14	24.66	33.19
c)	Other current assets	15	118.97	212.33
			3,339.50	**3,471.97**
Total Assets			**8,242.08**	**8,172.42**

			Note		
II)	**EQUITY AND LIABILITIES**				
	1)	**Equity**			
		a) Equity share capital	16	85.00	85.00
		b) Other equity	17	6,211.11	5,901.99
				6,296.11	**5,986.99**
	2)	**Liabilities**			
	i)	**Non-Current Liabilities**			
		a) Financial liabilities			
		(i) Lease liabilities		27.39	-
		(ii) Trade payables	18		
		Total outstanding dues of micro and small enterprises		-	-
		Total outstanding dues of creditors other than micro and small enterprises		5.74	4.79
		(iii) Other financial liabilities	19	2.95	2.26
		b) Provisions	20	63.78	45.16
		c) Deferred tax liabilities (net)	21	101.86	175.14
				201.72	**227.35**
	ii)	**Current Liabilities**			
		a) Financial liabilities			
		(i) Lease liabilities		0.61	-
		(ii) Trade payables	22		
		Total outstanding dues of micro and small enterprises		71.36	3.75
		Total outstanding dues of creditors other than micro and small enterprises		958.96	1,139.04
		(iii) Other financial liabilities	23	275.41	386.56
		b) Other current liabilities	24	141.49	160.26
		c) Provisions	25	296.42	268.47
				1,744.25	**1,958.08**
		Total Equity and Liabilities		**8,242.08**	**8,172.42**

The actual Balance Sheet of Exide Industries is shown on the last page. We will see the meaning and significance of each line item.

The sum of current and non-current liabilities are the total liabilities of a company.

In a balance sheet, assets are equal to liabilities plus shareholders equity. Shareholders equity is nothing else but company's net worth. So, to understand a company's net worth it is important to study its balance sheet.

So, knowing values of total assets and liabilities, we can find a company's net worth or shareholders equity which is total asset value less the liabilities.

In a balance sheet, there are always at least two columns that show all data for two consecutive periods. This helps in understanding a company's performance over these periods.

There is also a column called Notes. Detailed explanation of each data can be seen when by referring to the relevant note mentioned.

More the assets overweigh the liabilities, healthier is the company.

The first thing to notice is that the Balance Sheet is as on 31 Mar 2020 which means that this data is cumulative of all previous years which is unlike the P&L Statement that reflected data for one financial year only. Secondly, you will notice that all figures in crores of rupees. Thirdly, that total assets are equal to total equity and liabilities which is a feature of all Balance Sheets.

Non-Current Assets

Let us first look at the non-current assets also called fixed assets in the Balance Sheet.

1)	Non-Current Assets			
a)	Property, plant and equipment	2(a)	2,275.48	2,265.97
b)	Capital work-in-progress	2(a)	296.88	254.93
c)	Investment property	2(b)	34.23	-
d)	Right-of-use asset	2(c)	27.44	-
e)	Intangible assets	3	36.47	31.30
f)	Financial assets			
	(i) Investments	4	2,052.07	1,945.48
	(ii) Trade receivables	5	0.10	0.18
	(iii) Loans	6	17.19	18.18
g)	Current tax assets (net)		64.72	88.62
h)	Other non-current assets	7	98.00	95.79
			4,902.58	**4,700.45**

The first line item is property, plant and equipment which accounts for Rs 2,275.48 crores. Note 2(a) gives details:

2 (a) PROPERTY, PLANT AND EQUIPMENT

(Rs. in Crores)

	Freehold land	Land under Finance lease	Buildings (including roads)	Plant and equipment (including electrical installation)	Moulds	Office Equipment	Furniture & fittings	Vehicles	Computers	Total
Gross carrying amount										
Balance as at April1, 2018	33.56	73.47	411.58	1,714.10	233.48	13.59	5.01	2.39	23.39	2,510.57
Additions for the year 2018-19	20.57	0.17	82.88	467.40	66.50	2.91	0.77	0.24	11.87	653.31
Disposals / deductions for the year 2018-19	10.28	-	2.88	7.82	0.11	0.13	0.02	0.01	0.29	21.54
Balance as at March 31, 2019	**43.85**	**73.64**	**491.58**	**2,173.68**	**299.87**	**16.37**	**5.76**	**2.62**	**34.97**	**3,142.34**
Additions for the year 2019-20	6.71	-	40.54	288.74	29.35	5.26	0.76	0.63	8.08	380.07
Disposals / deductions for the year 2019-20	-	-	4.57	3.62	0.36	0.42	0.03	1.02	0.82	10.84
Reclassification to investment property	13.64	-	2.92	-	-	-	-	-	-	16.56
Balance as at March 31, 2020	**36.92**	**73.64**	**524.63**	**2,458.80**	**328.86**	**21.21**	**6.49**	**2.23**	**42.23**	**3,495.01**
Accumulated Depreciation										
Balance as at April1, 2018	-	2.03	35.53	457.37	62.44	5.81	0.71	1.20	10.51	575.60
Depreciation for the year 2018-19	-	1.96	17.39	244.23	30.91	2.62	0.49	0.42	7.11	305.13
Disposals / deductions for the year 2018-19	-	-	0.19	3.77	0.08	0.10	0.01	0.01	0.20	4.36
Balance as at March 31, 2019	**-**	**3.99**	**52.73**	**697.83**	**93.27**	**8.33**	**1.19**	**1.61**	**17.42**	**876.37**
Depreciation for the year 2019-20	-	1.97	22.96	278.24	35.08	2.76	0.59	0.33	8.67	350.60
Disposals / deductions for the year 2019-20	-	-	4.15	1.46	0.05	0.32	0.02	0.77	0.60	7.37
Reclassification to investment property	-	-	0.07	-	-	-	-	-	-	0.07
Balance as at March 31, 2020	**-**	**5.96**	**71.47**	**974.61**	**128.30**	**10.77**	**1.76**	**1.17**	**25.49**	**1,219.53**
Carrying amount (net)										
Balance as at March 31, 2019	43.85	69.65	438.85	1,475.85	206.60	8.04	4.57	1.01	17.55	2,265.97
Balance as at March 31, 2020	36.92	67.68	453.16	1,484.19	200.56	10.44	4.73	1.06	16.74	2,275.48

a. Conveyance / Lease deeds for certain immovable properties valued at Rs. 39.91 crs (PY: Rs. 41.31 crs) are pending execution.
b. Buildings includes Rs. 0.10 crs (PY: Rs. 0.10 crs) being the cost of shares in respective Co-operative Housing Societies.
c. Movement of capital work-in-progress:

	Opening Balance	Addition during the year	Capitalised	Closing Balance
2019-20	254.93	441.83	399.88	296.88
2018-19	233.50	674.21	652.78	254.93

Here, the data is divided into three parts, Gross Carrying Amount, Accumulated Depreciation and Net Carrying Amount. All the three parts show balance figures as at 31 Mar 2019 as well as at 31 Mar 2020 against each category of fixed asset like freehold land, land under finance lease, buildings including roads, etc.

For the current year, the net carrying amount is Rs 2,275.48 crores which is the total of all current assets after allowing for depreciation of Rs 1,219.53 crores.

For a little more understanding, let us study the data shown under plant and equipment after which it can be applied to every other fixed asset.

The gross carrying amount is the amortised of an asset before making any allowable deductions. Accumulated depreciation is the cumulative depreciation of an asset since its first use. The net carrying amount is the difference between gross carrying amount and the accumulated depreciation. The net carrying amount is also called the book value of the asset.

2 (a)   PROPERTY, PLANT AND EQUIPMENT

	Freehold land	Land under Finance lease	Buildings (including roads)	Plant and equipment (including electrical installation)
Gross carrying amount				
Balance as at April1, 2018	33.56	73.47	411.58	1,714.10
Additions for the year 2018-19	20.57	0.17	82.88	467.40
Disposals / deductions for the year 2018-19	10.28	-	2.88	7.82
Balance as at March 31, 2019	**43.85**	**73.64**	**491.58**	**2,173.68**
Additions for the year 2019-20	6.71	-	40.54	288.74
Disposals / deductions for the year 2019-20	-	-	4.57	3.62
Reclassification to investment property	13.64	-	2.92	-
Balance as at March 31, 2020	**36.92**	**73.64**	**524.63**	**2,458.80**
Accumulated Depreciation				
Balance as at April1, 2018	-	2.03	35.53	457.37
Depreciation for the year 2018-19	-	1.96	17.39	244.23
Disposals / deductions for the year 2018-19	-	-	0.19	3.77
Balance as at March 31, 2019	**-**	**3.99**	**52.73**	**697.83**
Depreciation for the year 2019-20	-	1.97	22.96	278.24
Disposals / deductions for the year 2019-20	-	-	4.15	1.46
Reclassification to investment property	-	-	0.07	-
Balance as at March 31, 2020	**-**	**5.96**	**71.47**	**974.61**
Carrying amount (net)				
Balance as at March 31, 2019	43.85	69.65	438.85	1,475.85
Balance as at March 31, 2020	36.92	67.68	453.16	1,484.19

Under the last column for plant and equipment, the gross carrying amount balance as at 1 Apr 2018 is shown Rs 1,714.10 crores. Additions made during the year are for Rs 467.40 crores, Rs 7.82 crores are for disposal / deductions. Thus, all add up to Rs 2,173.68 as balance as at 31 Mar 2019.

Similarly, additions made during the year 2019-20 are for Rs 288.74 crores, Rs 3.62 crores are for disposal / deductions. Thus, all these add up to a balance of Rs 2,458.80 as balance as at 31 Mar 2020.

Accumulated Depreciation is also worked out in a similar manner. The balance as on 31 Mar 2020 is Rs 974.61 crores. The net carrying amount as balance on 31 Mar 2020 is obtained by subtracting the accumulated depreciation balance as on 31 Mar 2020 from the gross carrying amount balance as at 31 Mar 2020, that is (2,458.80-974.61) = Rs 1,484.19 crores.

The next line item under the non-current assets relates to capital work in progress of Rs 296.88 crores. This is the cost incurred by the company to date against an asset whose work is not complete but still in progress.

A sum of Rs 34.23 crores is shown as a line item against investment property and Note 2(b) explains this.

2 (b)   INVESTMENT PROPERTY

	(Rs. in Crores)
	Land and Building
Gross carrying amount	
Balance as at April 1, 2019	-
Reclassification from property, plant and equipment	16.56
Additions for the year 2019-20	18.09
Balance as at March 31, 2020	**34.65**
Accumulated depreciation	
Balance as at April 1, 2019	-
Reclassification from property, plant and equipment	0.07
Depreciation for the year 2019-20	0.35
Balance as at March 31, 2020	**0.42**
Carrying amount (net)	
Balance as at March 31, 2020	34.23
Fair value of the investment property	34.65

This pertains to land and building which has been leased to subsidiary, Exide Leclanche Energy Private Limited and therefore treated as Investment Property. The fair value of investment property has been determined by external independent valuers.

The net carrying amount is similarly obtained as explained earlier. The item reclassification from property, plant and equipment means that the asset has undergone a new classification, or its usage has been changed. In this case the land and building has been leased to a subsidiary.

The next line item under non-current assets is right of use asset for which Rs 27.44 crores are shown. Note 2(c) explains the details.

As explained earlier, right of use asset is an asset which is not owned by the company but is used by it on lease basis. The net carrying amount as balance as on 31 Mar 2020 of Rs 27.44 is simple.

2 (c)   RIGHT-OF-USE ASSET

(Rs. in Crores)

	Plant and equipment
Gross carrying amount	
Balance as at April 01, 2019	-
Additions for the year 2019-20	28.58
Balance as at March 31, 2020	**28.58**
Accumulated depreciation	
Balance as at April 01, 2019	-
Depreciation for the year 2019-20	1.14
Balance as at March 31, 2020	**1.14**
Carrying amount (net)	
Balance as at March 31, 2020	**27.44**

The next line item against non-current assets is intangible assets against which Rs 36.47 crores are shown and Note 3 explains the details.

3   GOODWILL AND OTHER INTANGIBLE ASSETS

(Rs. in Crores)

	Goodwill	Trade Mark	Computer Software	Total
Gross carrying amount				
Balance as at April 1, 2018	3.89	3.12	41.26	48.27
Additions for the year 2018-19	-	-	16.31	16.31
Disposals / deductions for the year 2018-19	-	-	-	-
Balance as at March 31, 2019	**3.89**	**3.12**	**57.57**	**64.58**
Additions for the year 2019-20	-	-	15.71	15.71
Disposals / deductions for the year 2019-20	-	-	-	-
Balance as at March 31, 2020	**3.89**	**3.12**	**73.28**	**80.29**
Accumulated amortisation & impairment losses				
Balance as at April 1, 2018	3.89	2.37	18.65	24.91
Amortisation for the year 2018-19	-	0.53	7.84	8.37
Balance as at March 31, 2019	**3.89**	**2.90**	**26.49**	**33.28**
Amortisation for the year 2019-20		0.22	10.32	10.54
Balance as at March 31, 2020	**3.89**	**3.12**	**36.81**	**43.82**
Carrying amount (net)				
Balance as at March 31, 2019	-	0.22	31.08	31.30
Balance as at March 31, 2020	-	-	36.47	36.47

Intangible assets in this case are goodwill, trademark and computer software, and the net carrying amount as balance on 31 Mar 2020 is Rs 36.47 crores. Amortisation is equivalent to depreciation in case of tangible assets.

The next line item is financial assets under non-current assets, and under it we have investments of Rs 2052.07 crores, trade receivables of Rs 0.10 crores and loans of Rs 17.19 crores. Notes 4, 5 and 6 give the details.

4 NON-CURRENT INVESTMENTS

(Rs. in Crores)

	March 31, 2020	March 31, 2019
Investments at cost (unquoted)		
Equity Shares, Fully Paid Up		
In Subsidiary Companies		
Chloride International Limited of Rs. 10 each [4,50,000 shares (PY: 4,50,000 Shares)]	0.20	0.20
Chloride Power Systems and Solutions Limited of Rs. 10 each [19,80,000 shares (PY:19,80,000 Shares)]	2.93	2.93
Chloride Metals Limited of Rs. 10 each [4,73,80,952 shares (PY: 4,73,80,952 shares)]	144.03	144.03
Chloride Batteries S.E.Asia Pte Limited of Singapore $ 1 each [70,00,000 shares (PY: 70,00,000 shares)]	10.35	10.35
Espex Batteries Limited of GBP 1 each [1,02,000 shares (PY: 1,02,000 shares)]	0.78	0.78
Associated Battery Manufacturers (Ceylon) Ltd of Sri Lankan Rupees 10 each [38,96,640 shares (PY: 38,96,640 shares)]	7.31	7.31
Exide Life Insurance Company Limited of Rs. 10 each [185,00,00,000 shares (PY: 185,00,00,000 shares)]	1,679.59	1,679.59
Exide Leclanche Energy Private Limited of Rs. 10 each [7,65,30,920 shares (PY: 4,12,81,995 shares)]	125.88	41.28
In Associate Companies		
CSE Solar Sunpark Maharashtra Private Limited of Rs. 10 each [9,92,465 shares (PY: NIL)]	7.24	-
CSE Solar Sunpark Tamil Nadu Private Limited of Rs. 10 each [11,81,250 shares (PY: NIL)]	10.87	-
Greenyana Solar Private Limited of Rs. 10 each [5,83,333 shares (PY: NIL)]	5.25	-
Investments at amortised cost		
Government Securities (lodged as security deposits with various authorities)	0.01	0.01
	March 31, 2020	March 31, 2019
Investments at fair value through OCI		
Debentures (fully paid up)		
Woodlands Multispeciality Hospital Limited		
1/2% Debentures of Rs. 100 each [20 debentures (PY: 20 debentures)]	-	- ^
5% Non-redeemable Registered Debentures of Rs. 6000 each (1 debenture (PY: 1 debenture)	-	- ^
UNITS (UNQUOTED)		
Fearing Capital India Evolving Fund of Rs. 1000 each [4,01,696 units (PY: 3,03,406 units)]	46.37	40.71
EQUITY SHARES (UNQUOTED)		
Haldia Integrated Development Agency Ltd of Rs. 10 each [5,00,000 shares [PY: 5,00,000 shares)]	2.15	2.45
Suryadev Alloys of Rs. 10 each [5,80,000 shares (PY: 2,500 shares)]	1.76	0.03
EQUITY SHARES (QUOTED)		
Hathway Cable and Datacom Limited of Rs. 2 each [54,62,830 shares (PY: 54,62,830 shares)]	7.35	15.81
	2,052.07	**1,945.48**
(i) Aggregate book value of unquoted investments	2,044.72	1,929.67
(ii) Aggregate value of quoted investments and market value thereof	7.35	15.81
(iii) Refer Note 41 for information about fair value measurement and Note 42 for credit risk and market risk of investment		
(iv) ^ Figures being less than Rs. 50,000 in each case, has not been disclosed		

Non-current investments are long term investments that the company has made for which the full value will not be realised during the accounting year. The company's investments are self-explanatory.

5 NON-CURRENT TRADE RECEIVABLES (AT AMORTISED COST)

(Rs. in Crores)

	March 31, 2020	March 31, 2019
Trade receivables, considered good - unsecured	0.10	0.18
	0.10	**0.18**

Non-current trade receivables are of Rs 0.10 crores. Non-current trade receivables refer to goods or services sold on credit by the company.

6 NON-CURRENT LOANS (AT AMORTISED COST)

(Rs. in Crores)

	March 31, 2020	March 31, 2019
Unsecured, considered good		
a) Loans to employees	0.01	-
b) Loans and advances to others	0.01	0.01
c) Security deposits	17.17	18.17
	17.19	**18.18**

Non-current loans are loans given by the company receipts of which are not expected during the year. Here the company has given loans to its employees, loans and advances to others and made a security deposit all totalling to Rs 17.19 crores.

Under non-current assets, the next line item relates to net current tax assets of Rs 64.72 crores. These are excess taxes that have been paid during the year but are no refund is expected.

The last line item under non-current assets is other non-current assets of Rs 98.00 crores. Note 7 provides the details.

7   OTHER NON-CURRENT ASSETS

		(Rs. in Crores)	
		March 31, 2020	March 31, 2019
(i) Unsecured, considered good			
a)	Capital advances	40.58	41.16
b)	Prepaid expenses	39.87	37.52
c)	Balances and deposit with Government Authorities	17.55	17.10
(ii) Unsecured, considered doubtful			
a)	Advances recoverable in cash or kind	1.79	2.04
b)	Balances and deposit with Government Authorities	24.94	22.52
		124.73	**120.34**
	Less: Provision for doubtful advances	26.73	24.55
		98.00	**95.79**

Capital advances are amounts given by a company as advance for procurement of a non-current asset. Prepaid are payments made for future expenses in advance. Rest of the lines are self-explanatory.

The total of all non-current assets is shown as Rs 4,902.58 crores.

Current Assets

Now let us look at the Current Assets that can be easily converted to cash with 365 days. Such assets are inventories, financial assets like investments, trade receivables, cash and cash equivalents, bank balances, loans and other financial assets.

Notes 8, 9, 10, 11, 12, 13, 14 and 15 explain these respectively.

			4,902.58	4,700.45
2)	**Current Assets**			
	a) Inventories	8	2,192.27	1,803.97
	b) Financial assets			
	(i) Investments	9	18.73	253.91
	(ii) Trade receivables	10	815.30	1,081.04
	(iii) Cash and cash equivalents	11	144.87	64.70
	(iv) Bank balances other than (iii) above	12	9.72	8.85
	(v) Loans	13	14.98	13.98
	(vi) Other financial assets	14	24.66	33.19
	c) Other current assets	15	118.97	212.33
			3,339.50	**3,471.97**
Total Assets			**8,242.08**	**8,172.42**

Here all item lines are self-explanatory except the line items referred as inventories, cash and cash equivalents and bank balances other than cash and cash equivalents.

Inventories are goods and raw materials that are ready for sale. Note 8 is self-explanatory.

8 INVENTORIES

			(Rs. in Crores)
		March 31, 2020	March 31, 2019
(At lower of cost and net realisable value)			
a)	Stores, spare parts, loose tools, etc.	46.33	43.37
b)	Raw materials and components [Including in transit/ lying in bonded warehouse Rs. 176.08 crs (PY: Rs. 120.77 crs)]	577.40	451.64
c)	Work-in-progress	707.76	530.04
d)	Finished goods	854.28	773.68
e)	Stock-in-trade	6.50	5.24
		2,192.27	**1,803.97**

I. The cost of inventories recognised as an expense during the year has been disclosed on the face of the Statement of Profit and Loss and Note 33.

II. The cost of inventories recognised as an expense includes Rs. 16.72 crs (PY: Rs. 12.00 crs) in respect of write downs of inventory.

Cash and cash equivalents refer to cash and securities that can be easily converted to cash. Note 11 explains.

11 CASH AND CASH EQUIVALENTS

			(Rs. in Crores)
		March 31, 2020	March 31, 2019
a)	Balances with banks on		
	Current account	144.67	64.42
b)	Cash in hand	0.20	0.28
		144.87	**64.70**

Bank balances other than cash and cash equivalents are basically amounts with the company that does not belong to them and may be claimed at short notice. In this case it is an amount of Rs 9.72 crores that is with the company as unclaimed dividend by investors. Note 12 shows this clearly.

12 BANK BALANCES OTHER THAN CASH AND CASH EQUIVALENTS

		(Rs. in Crores)
	March 31, 2020	March 31, 2019
Unclaimed dividend account	9.72	8.85
	9.72	**8.85**

The total of all current assets is Rs 3,339.50 crores, and the total of non-current and current assets is Rs 8,242.08 crores.

Equity & Liabilities

This segment of the balance sheet is in two parts, equity and liabilities. In the first segment of the balance sheet, we saw the assets that the company has, whereas this segment explains how the assets have been financed.

II)	EQUITY AND LIABILITIES			
1)	Equity			
	a) Equity share capital	16	85.00	85.00
	b) Other equity	17	6,211.11	5,901.99
			6,296.11	**5,986.99**
2)	Liabilities			
i)	Non-Current Liabilities			
	a) Financial liabilities			
	(i) Lease liabilities		27.39	-
	(ii) Trade payables	18		
	Total outstanding dues of micro and small enterprises		-	-
	Total outstanding dues of creditors other than micro and small enterprises		5.74	4.79
	(iii) Other financial liabilities	19	2.95	2.26
	b) Provisions	20	63.78	45.16
	c) Deferred tax liabilities (net)	21	101.86	175.14
			201.72	**227.35**
ii)	Current Liabilities			
	a) Financial liabilities			
	(i) Lease liabilities		0.61	-
	(ii) Trade payables	22		
	Total outstanding dues of micro and small enterprises		71.36	3.75
	Total outstanding dues of creditors other than micro and small enterprises		958.96	1,139.04
	(iii) Other financial liabilities	23	275.41	386.56
	b) Other current liabilities	24	141.49	160.26
	c) Provisions	25	296.42	268.47
			1,744.25	**1,958.08**
	Total Equity and Liabilities		**8,242.08**	**8,172.42**

The first item line under Equity is equity share capital of Rs 85 crores. Details can be understood from Note 16.

16 SHARE CAPITAL

			(Rs. in Crores)
		March 31, 2020	March 31, 2019
a)	**Authorised**		
	100,00,00,000 (PY: 100,00,00,000) equity shares of Re. 1 each	100.00	100.00
		100.00	100.00
b)	**Issued, subscribed & fully paid-up**		
	85,00,00,000 (PY: 85,00,00,000) equity shares of Re. 1 each	85.00	85.00
		85.00	85.00
c)	**Reconciliation of the number of equity shares outstanding at the beginning and at the end of the reporting year**		
	Balance at the beginning and at the end of the year	85,00,00,000	85,00,00,000
d)	**Terms / rights attached to equity shares**		

The company has only one class of equity shares having a par value of Re. 1 per share. Each holder of equity shares is entitled to one vote per share.

In the event of liquidation of the Company, the holders of equity shares will be entitled to receive remaining assets of the company, after distribution of all preferential amounts. The distribution will be in proportion to the number of equity shares held by the shareholders.

e)	**Shares held by holding company**		
	Name of shareholder		
	Chloride Eastern Limited, UK (considered to be Holding company by virtue of de-facto control) 45.99% (PY: 45.99%)	39,09,54,666	39,09,54,666

f)	**Details of shareholders holding more than 5% shares in Company**		
	Name of shareholder		**Number of Shares**
	Chloride Eastern Limited, UK holding 45.99% (PY: 45.99%)	39,09,54,666	39,09,54,666

As per records of the company, including its register of shareholders / members and other declaration received from shareholders, the above shareholding represents legal ownership of shares.

The authorised share capital is the number of shares the company is allowed to issue. In this case, the company is allowed to issue 100 crore shares each of Re 1 as face value.

The company has also issued, subscribed & fully paid-up shares worth 85 crores. This means that out of 100 crores worth of authorised shares, the company has issued shares worth 85 crores which have been fully subscribed and cash received.

The company also reports that they have reconciled this figure of 85 crore shares at the beginning and at the end of the year. Since the figure is same, there is no mismatch.

The company also tells us that out of the 85 crore shares that are issued, its holding company Chloride Eastern Ltd has 39,09,54,666 shares, that is 45.99% of 85 crore issued shares.

The company also provides details of shareholders who own more than 5% of shares. In this case, it is only the holding company which is holding more than 5% of issued shares.

The second line item under Equity is other equity of value Rs 6,211.11 crores. For details we will refer to Note 17.

17 OTHER EQUITY

		March 31, 2020	March 31, 2019
			(Rs. in Crores)
a)	**Securities premium**	737.88	737.88
	Premium received on equity shares issued is recognised in the securities premium		
b)	**Retained earnings**	5,470.53	5,151.98
	Retained earnings are profits that the Company has earned till date, less dividends or other distributions paid to the shareholders. It also includes remeasurement gain/ loss of defined benefit plans.		
c)	**Items of Other Comprehensive Income**		
	- Fair value of equity instruments through OCI	2.70	12.13
	Changes in fair value of equity instruments recorded in other comprehensive income		
		6,211.11	**5,901.99**

Securities premium amount is shown as Rs 737.88 crores. This is the difference between the issue price and the face value of shares. This arises when the company issue shares for the first time.

Retained earnings are portion of earnings left with the company after payment of dividends. In this case it is Rs 5,470.53 crores.

Items of other comprehensive income refers to revenue, expenses, gains or losses that are yet to be realised and not included in the net income of a P&L Account. In this case, the company has shown an income of Rs 2.70

crores as fair value of equity instruments that they hold.

The total income from other equity is shown as Rs 6,211.11 crores. When this amount is added to the equity capital of 85 crores, the total income from Equity is (6,211.11+85.00) = Rs 6,296.11 crores.

Now we will look at the Liabilities.

Liabilities

Here liability is what the company owes to others. Liabilities are also divided under two heads, non-current and current.

Non-current liabilities are long term liabilities the dues of which are more than a year away.

Current liabilities are liabilities that are short term the dues of which are to be paid within a year.

Let us firstly see the non-current liabilities the company has.

i) Non-Current Liabilities			
a) Financial liabilities			
(i) Lease liabilities		27.39	.
(ii) Trade payables	18		
Total outstanding dues of micro and small enterprises		.	.
Total outstanding dues of creditors other than micro and small enterprises		5.74	4.79
(iii) Other financial liabilities	19	2.95	2.26
b) Provisions	20	63.78	45.16
c) Deferred tax liabilities (net)	21	101.86	175.14
		201.72	**227.35**

The total non-current liabilities are Rs 201.72 crores which is made up of lease liability of Rs 27.39 crores, Rs 5.74 crores as total outstanding dues to creditors, Rs 2.95 crores as other financial liability, Rs 63.78 crores against provisions and Rs 101.86 crores towards deferred tax liability.

Lease liability is the obligation for the company to pay against assets that have been given to them on lease.

Outstanding dues to creditors are self-explanatory.

Details of other financial liabilities is given in Note 19 which is again self-explanatory.

19 OTHER NON-CURRENT FINANCIAL LIABILITIES (AT AMORTISED COST)

	(Rs. in Crores)	
	March 31, 2020	March 31, 2019
Payable for capital goods	2.95	2.26
	2.95	**2.26**

Provisions are amounts that are kept for uncertain payments that may be required to be paid. In this case the company has earmarked an amount of Rs 63.78 crores. For details Note 20 can be seen.

20 NON CURRENT PROVISIONS

	(Rs. in Crores)	
	March 31, 2020	March 31, 2019
Provision for employee benefits (refer note 36)		
Post retirement medical benefits	4.55	4.27
Gratuity	17.84	3.97
Pension	3.42	3.62
Compensated absences	36.44	31.92
Others		
Provision for site restoration liabilities	1.53	1.38
	63.78	**45.16**

All the line items are self-explanatory here.

Deferred tax liabilities are taxes that are due but not paid. The company has provisioned an amount of Rs 101.16 crores. Note 21 gives the details.

21 DEFERRED TAX LIABILITY (NET)

	(Rs. in Crores)	
	March 31, 2020	March 31, 2019
Deferred tax liabilities	136.22	212.06
Less: Deferred tax assets	34.36	36.92
	101.86	**175.14**

When a company foresees that its depreciation methodology may be questioned by the tax authorities, it resorts to provisioning of deferred tax liabilities.

So, in the last line we see that the total non-current liabilities are Rs 201.72 crores.

Now, let us examine the current liabilities which are a total of Rs 1,744.25 crores.

ii)	Current Liabilities			
	a) Financial liabilities			
	(i) Lease liabilities		0.61	-
	(ii) Trade payables	22		
	Total outstanding dues of micro and small enterprises		71.36	3.75
	Total outstanding dues of creditors other than micro and small enterprises		958.96	1,139.04
	(iii) Other financial liabilities	23	275.41	386.56
	b) Other current liabilities	24	141.49	160.26
	c) Provisions	25	296.42	268.47
			1,744.25	**1,958.08**
	Total Equity and Liabilities		**8,242.08**	**8,172.42**

Similar to non-current liabilities, here too there is a lease liability of Rs

0.61 crores; outstanding due to small and micro enterprises of Rs 71.36 crores; outstanding due to other creditors of Rs 958.96 crores; Rs 275.41 crores towards other financial liabilities; Rs141.49 against other current liabilities; and Rs 296.42 crores towards provisions.

Note 23 gives details of other financial liabilities.

23 OTHER CURRENT FINANCIAL LIABILITIES (AT AMORTISED COST)

		(Rs. in Crores)	
		March 31, 2020	March 31, 2019
a)	Unclaimed dividends (to be credited to Investor Education and Protection Fund as and when due)	9.72	8.85
b)	Other payables -		
	For selling and distribution costs	143.96	236.10
	For capital goods	53.63	83.14
	For other expenses *	68.10	58.47
		275.41	**386.56**

Note 24 gives details of other current liabilities. All lines are self-explanatory.

24 OTHER CURRENT LIABILITIES

		(Rs. in Crores)	
		March 31, 2020	March 31, 2019
a)	Taxes and duties payable	52.25	106.00
b)	Advances from customers	29.90	18.22
c)	Deferred revenue *	59.34	36.04
		141.49	**160.26**

* Deferred revenue relates to loyalty credit points granted to the customers as part of sales transactions and has been estimated with reference to the fair value of the products for which they could be redeemed.

Note 25 gives details of provisions which are also self-explanatory.

25 CURRENT PROVISIONS

		(Rs. in Crores)	
		March 31, 2020	March 31, 2019
a)	Provision for employee benefits (refer Note 36)		
	Post retirement medical benefits	0.38	0.35
	Compensated absences	2.20	2.62
b)	Others		
	Provision for warranty claims	239.65	211.31
	Provision for litigation's and tax disputes	54.19	54.19
		296.42	**268.47**

Provisions for warranties

A provision is recognised for expected warranty claims on products sold, based on past experience of the level of repairs and returns. The table below gives information about movement in warranty provision:

	March 31, 2020	March 31, 2019
Opening balance	211.31	175.18
Add: Provision created during the year	269.64	261.98
Less: Utilised against warranty claims during the year	241.30	225.85
Closing balance	**239.65**	**211.31**

Provisions for litigations and tax disputes

The management has estimated the provisions for pending litigation, claims and demands relating to indirect taxes based on its assessment of probability for these demands crystallising against the company in due course:

	March 31, 2020	March 31, 2019
Opening balance	54.19	54.19
Add: Provision created during the year	-	-
Closing balance	**54.19**	**54.19**

When we add the total current liabilities of Rs 1,744.25 crores to Rs 201.72 crores of non-current liabilities and Rs 6,296.11 of equity capital we have a net liability of Rs 8,242.08 crores. This amount is equal to net assets of Rs 8,242.08 crores.

UNDERSTANDING CASH FLOW STATEMENTS

Cash Flow Statements help investors to understand how efficiently the company is managing its cash and in assessing liquidity and solvency. Cash flow statements, like P&L accounts, reflect data for a financial year

The three main components of a cash flow statement are:

1. **Cash from Operating Activities.** All cash inflows and outflows resulting from revenue generating activities are shown here. These could be related to sales, marketing, purchase of raw materials, cost of labour, advertising, shipping, etc.

2. **Cash from Investing Activities.** All inflows and outflows relating to investments made by the company like purchase of machinery or property or a new business, investments, etc.

3. **Cash from Financial Activities.** This relates to inflows from investors and banks as well as outflows with respect to dividends paid to investors, interest payments to banks, issuing corporate bonds, etc.

Each activity that a company undertakes can be classified under one of the above mentioned three categories, and each activity the company undertakes involves the movement of cash, either in or out. Some activities generate tangible or intangible assets.

When a company's liabilities increase, cash balance will also increase. When assets of a company increase, cash balance decreases.

The sum of all cash flows indicates how much is the company's cash inflow or outflow.

Generally, a company whose cash flow from operating activities show an increasing trend is considered a healthy sign.

In a cash flow statement, there are always at least two columns that show all data for two consecutive periods. This helps in understanding a company's performance over these periods.

Let us now see an actual Cash Flow Statement of Exide Industries.

Statement of Cash Flows
for the year ended 31st March 2020

		2019-20		2018-19	(Rs. in Crores)
(A)	**CASH FLOW FROM OPERATING ACTIVITIES:**				
	Net profit before tax		1,035.19		1,238.58
	Adjustment for:				
	Depreciation and amortisation	362.63		313.60	
	Loss on property, plant and equipment sold / discarded (net)	2.07		0.34	
	Exceptional items	-		(108.29)	
	Dividend income	(37.15)		(17.86)	
	Rent income	(2.17)		(0.05)	
	Interest income	(5.73)		(3.81)	
	Gain on fair valuation of investments designated as FVTPL	(0.42)		(0.48)	
	Finance costs	9.40		6.05	
	Provision for expected credit loss / (write-back)	14.74		(4.09)	
			343.37		185.31
	Operating profit before working capital changes		**1,378.56**		**1,423.89**
	(Increase)/decrease in trade receivables	251.08		(132.56)	
	(Increase) in inventories	(388.31)		(43.82)	
	(Increase) / decrease in other financial assets, loans and other assets	99.09		(13.14)	
	Increase/(decrease) in financial liabilities, other liabilities and provisions	(177.37)	(215.51)	142.73	(46.79)
	Cash generated from operations		**1,163.05**		**1,377.10**
	Direct taxes paid (net of refunds and interest thereon)		(249.42)		(373.31)
	Net cash generated from operating activities		**913.63**		**1,003.79**
(B)	**CASH FLOW FROM INVESTING ACTIVITIES:**				
	Purchase and construction of property, plant and equipment (including intangible assets)	(465.98)		(676.08)	
	Proceeds from sale of property, plant and equipment	1.41		125.12	
	Acquisition of investment property	(18.09)		-	
	Investment in subsidiary	(84.60)		(176.27)	
	Investment in associates	(23.36)		-	
	Acquisition of investment in shares/units	(14.37)		(8.16)	
	Redemption of investment in shares/units	4.27		0.24	
	Purchase of investment of mutual fund units	(1,535.00)		(1,140.00)	
	Sale of investment of mutual fund units	1,770.00		1,090.00	
	Interest received	0.94		0.71	
	Rent received	2.17		0.05	
	Dividend received	37.74		18.78	
	Net cash used in investing activities		**(324.87)**		**(765.61)**
(C)	**CASH FLOW FROM FINANCING ACTIVITIES:**				
	Dividends paid (including tax)	(498.61)		(245.94)	
	Payment of lease liabilities	(3.03)		-	
	Interest paid	(6.95)		(6.05)	
	Net cash used in financing activities		**(508.59)**		**(251.99)**
	Net increase / (decrease) in cash and cash equivalents (A+B+C)		80.17		(13.81)
	Cash and cash equivalents - opening balance #		64.70		78.51
	Cash and cash equivalents - closing balance #		**144.87**		**64.70**

The first thing to note that a cash flow statement is for the year ended on 31 Mar 2020 which means that the figures contained in the statement refer to the financial year 2019-20. The second thing to note is that all figures mentioned in the statement are in crores of rupees.

The statement is divided into three parts, cash flow from operating activities, cash flow from investing activities and cash flow from financing activities. Each line item is self-explanatory and needs no real explanation.

Point to note is that the net cash generated from operating activities is

Rs 913.63 crores which is less than the previous year's figure of Rs 1,003.79 crores. However, a positive cash flow from operating activities is considered healthy for a company as this cash has come into the company.

The cash flow from investing activities is Rs (324.87) crores. As the figure is negative, it means that the cash has gone out of the company implying that the company is using its cash wisely.

The cash flow from financing activities is Rs (508.59) crores. Here again, the figure is negative which means that this cash has gone out of the company, the largest component being payment of dividends of Rs (498.61) crores.

We also notice that the net cash flow during the financial year 2019-20 is Rs 80.17 crores, and the net cash flow for the financial year 2018-19 is Rs (13.81) crores. This means that the company during the year 2019-20 received Rs 80.17 into the company, compared to Rs 13.81 crores that went out of the company during 2018-19.

Analysing Financial Statements

Analysing financial statements is akin to carrying out complete health check-up of a person to find if everything is all right or not. You should be interested basically in companies that exhibit a growing trend on revenue, PAT, EPS, gross profit margins and return on equity; a low debt level; fast moving inventory and quick receivables in case the company is a manufacturing unit; and positive cash flows from operations. All these factors must be analysed over a period of at least 5 years. Let us see how these parameters can be analysed:

1. **Revenue & PAT Growth.** Investing in companies that are growing their revenues and profit at more than 15% CAGR can be beneficial. To calculate revenue and PAT growth CAGR, we must first calculate the annual rate of growth.

	FY 2015-16	FY 2016-17	FY2017-18	FY 2018-19	FY 2019-20
Revenue	6,848	7,583	9,186	10,588	9,857
Revenue Growth		10.7%	21.1%	15.3%	-6.9%

PAT	624	694	668	844	826
PAT Growth		11.2%	-3.7%	26.3%	-2.1%

Table 1

The above table shows how revenue and PAT has been growing over the last 5 years in Exide Industries.

Considering the above data, we see that the CAGR for revenue and PAT works out to 7.56% and 5.77% respectively, which is well below our expectation of 15%.

2. **Earnings Per Share.** The earnings per share of Exide Industries over a period of 5 years is:

	2015-16	2016-17	2017-18	2018-19	2019-20
Earnings per Share	7.35	8.16	7.86	9.93	9.71
Earnings per Share Growth		11.0%	-3.7%	26.3%	-2.2%
Share Capital	85	85	85	85	85

Table 2

Here, the CAGR of earning per share is 5.73% which is in line with PAT which is good.

3. **Gross Profit Margins.** For calculating the gross profit margin, we have to first calculate the cost of goods sold. The cost of goods is equal to the sum of cost of materials consumed plus the purchases of stock in trade plus expenses towards power and fuel. How this is to be calculated, I have explained in detail in the next chapter under Inventory Turnover Ratio.

Gross profit = (Net Sales – Cost of Goods Sold)

Data for Exide industries is as under:

	FY 2015-16	FY 2016-17	FY2017-18	FY 2018-19	FY 2019-20
Net Sales	6,848	7,583	9,186	10,588	9,857
Cost of goods sold	4,385	5,317	6,493	7,404	6,925
Gross Profits	2,463	2,266	2,693	3,184	2,932
Gross Profit	36.0%	29.9%	29.3%	30.1%	29.7%

Margins					

Table 3

Gross profit margins over 20% should be our expectation. Here, it is more than 20% which is quite healthy.

4. **Return on Equity.** This is of interest to you as it measures the return generated by the company on the shareholders equity. Let us examine Exide Industries' performance over the last 5 years.

	FY 2015-16	FY 2016-17	FY2017-18	FY 2018-19	FY 2019-20
PAT	624	694	688	844	826
Shareholder Equity	4,434	4,963	5,389	5,987	6,296
Return on Equity (ROE)	14.1%	14.0%	12.8%	14.1%	13.1%

Table 4

We see that in case of Exide Industries that the ROE is almost constant but below 20%. It is better to invest in companies that have an ROE greater than 20%.

5. **Debt Level.** A company that has a low debt to EBITDA ratios a good company. Given below is the data for Exide Industries that has almost negligible debt to EBITDA ratio.

	FY 2015-16	FY 2016-17	FY2017-18	FY 2018-19	FY 2019-20
Debt	102.5	170.23	0	0	28
EBITDA	906	1,186	1,299	1,449	1,428
Debt / EBITDA	11.3%	14.4%	0.0%	0.0%	2.0%

Table 5

6. **Inventory Check.** Here you need to check how much time is taken for sale to happen after the product is ready. If the inventory number of days shows a decline, it indicates efficiency. Also, inventory and PAT should show similar growth pattern. This we shall see in detail in the next chapter.

7. **Sales & Receivables.** The time taken between the date a sale is effective and receipt of cash thereon can tell you how efficient the sales team is. Therefore, the ratio of receivables / net sales in percentage terms

should show signs of decline. We shall see how to calculate this in the next chapter.

8. **Cash Flows from Operations.** A good company will have a positive cash flow from operations and exhibit a growing trend over a period. Positive cash flows from operations indicate that the company is generating cash. Let us see this for Exide Industries:

	FY 2015-16	FY 2016-17	FY2017-18	FY 2018-19	FY 2019-20
Cash Flow from Operations	1339.68	429.91	516.61	1003.79	913.63

Table 6

The table above shows that Exide Industries has generated positive cash flows over a period of 5 years which is a good sign.

By now we have understood what all the line items in a P&L Statement, Balance Sheet and the Cash Flow Statement convey to us and how to analyse these statements. However, we have not interpreted what these numbers mean to us. These numbers can be interpreted by using some of the financial ratios which we will see in the next chapter.

9 QUANTITATIVE ANALYSIS: FINANCIAL RATIOS

"An important key to investing is to remember that stocks are not lottery tickets"

Peter Lynch

For many reading and analysing financial reports can be quite a job, but this job can be made easy by understanding some key ratios derived out of financial statements. These ratios can be calculated by you or you can easily access them from sites such as money control, value research, screeners, etc.

There are several ratios and for better understanding, these ratios can broadly be covered loosely under following heads as some ratios overlap:

1. Profitability Ratios,

2. Leverage Ratios,

3. Valuation Ratios, and

4. Operational Ratios.

Ratios on their own convey very little. They are best understood when compared with similar ratios of similar companies or when you look into the financial ratio's trend over a period of at least 4 to 5 years.

Another point to remember is that companies use different accounting policies, and some change their accounting policies from year to year. If you notice this, then you need to adjust your data accordingly before you start calculating financial ratios. For better understanding, we should calculate the Compound Annual Growth rate (CAGR) for each ratio.

We will attempt to calculate some financial ratios from the Annual Report of Exide Industries Ltd for the financial year 2019-20.

Profitability Ratios

Profitability Ratios help the analyst to measure the company's profitability. Profits are needed for business expansion as well as paying dividends to shareholders. Let us see some of the profitability ratios, and what do they convey to us:

1. **EBITDA & EBITDA Margin.** EBITDA stands for Earnings Before Interest Tax Depreciation and Amortisation. To calculate EBITDA Margin, we have to firstly calculate EBITDA.

EBITDA = (Operating Revenues - Operating Expenses),

Operating Revenues = (Total Revenue - Other Income), and

Operating Expense = (Total Expense - Finance Cost - Depreciation & Amortisation Cost).

EBITDA Margin = EBITDA / (Total Revenue - Other Income)

EBITDA indicates how much money a company makes, and the EBITDA Margin is the percentage profitability of the company at the operating level.

Let us calculate the EBITDA & the EBITDA Margin for Exide Industries.

We know, from the Balance Sheet that operating revenues = (9,920.66 - 63.94) = Rs 9,856.66 crores, and operating expenses = (8,491.68 - 9.40 - 362.63) = Rs 8,119.65 crores. Therefore, EBITDA = (9,856.66 − 8,119.65) = Rs 1,737.01 crores.

EBITDA Margin = 1737.01 / 9856.66 = 0.18 or 18%.

2. **Profit After Tax (PAT) Margin.** The EBITDA Margin is calculated at the operational level, PAT Margin is calculated at the final profitability level taking into consideration all expenses and total revenues. Here, the PAT is explicitly mentioned in the Balance Sheet.

PAT Margin = (PAT / Total Revenues) expressed as a percentage.

PAT Margin indicates overall profitability of a company.

In the case of Exide Industries, from the P&L Statement PAT = 825.51 crores and total revenues = 9,920.60 crores.

Therefore, PAT Margin = 825.51 / 9920.60 = 0.08 or 8%

3. **Return on Equity (ROE).** This is an important ratio and considered seriously by analysts. It indicates how well the investors are being rewarded. Higher the number, better it is.

ROE = (Net Profit / Average Stockholder Equity) expressed as a percentage.

In the case of Exide Industries, Net Profit = Rs 825.51 crores, and the average stockholder equity = (6296.11 + 5986.99) / 2 = Rs 6,141.55 crores. Whenever, an average is to be taken, take figures of current and previous year can be considered.

Therefore, ROE = 825.51 / 6141.55 = 0.13 or 13%. This is a quick method of finding ROE.

Calculating ROE by the above method has its own drawback as it does not consider the debt the company carries. If the company carries a huge debt, its PAT Margin would be higher as well. To overcome this anomaly, use the DuPont Model also called the DuPont Identity. Using this model, the formula for ROE can be written as:

ROE = (Net Profit / Net Sales) x (Net Sales / Av Total Assets) x (Av Total Assets / Shareholder Equity)

The new formula considers the three components Net Profit Margin, Asset Turnover and Financial Leverage to calculate a more realistic ROE.

A low Net Profit Margin suggests higher input costs and increased competition.

A higher Asset Turnover ratio suggests that the assets are being used efficiently. If this ratio is low, it is an indication that there are management issues.

A high Financial Leverage ratio suggests that the company is highly leveraged, and the investor should get cautious.

In the case of Exide Industries, Net Profit = 825.51 crores, Net Sales = 9,856.66 crores, Average Total Assets = (8242.08 + 8172.42) / 2 = Rs 8,207.25 crores, and Shareholder Equity = 6,296.11 crores.

Therefore, Net Profit / Net Sales = 825.51 / 9856.66 = 0.08 or 8%; Net Sales / Average Total Assets = 9856.66 / 8207.25 = 1.20 times, and Average Total Assets / Shareholder Equity = 8207.25 / 6296.11 = 1.30 times

ROE = 0.08 * 1.2 * 1.3 = 0.125 or 12.5%

Invest in companies that have an ROE of more than 18%. Average ROE of good Indian companies lies between 14 to 16%. A high ROE coupled with a high debt is not a healthy sign.

4. **Return on Assets (ROA).** This ratio is used to evaluate a company's ability to use its assets to generate profits. In other words, it is the management's efficiency in deploying its assets. Higher the ratio, better it is.

ROA = [Net Income + Interest * (1 - Tax Rate)] / (Total Average Assets)

In the case of Exide Industries, Net Income = Profit for the year = Rs 825.51 crores, Total Average Assets = (8242.08 + 8172.42) / 2 = Rs 8,207.25 crores, Interest = Finance Cost = 9.40 crores, Tax rate = 32%, then

ROA = [825.51 + 9.4(1-0.32)] / 8207.25 = 0.10 or 10%

5. **Return on Capital Employed (ROCE).** This measures a company's profitability with respect to efficient employment of its capital. Higher the

number, better it is. Capital employed is sum of shareholders equity and debt liabilities.

ROCE = (Earnings Before Interest and Taxes / Overall Capital Employed)

ROCE indicates overall return a company generates considering equity, long and short-term debts.

In the case of Exide Industries, Earnings Before Interest and Taxes = 1,428.92 crores, Overall Capital Employed = Short Term Debt + Long Term Debt + Equity = (275.41+2.95+6296.11) = Rs 6,574.47 crores, then

ROCE = 1428.92 / 6574.47 = 0.22 or 22%

Leverage Ratios

Leverage Ratios are also called Solvency Ratios as they assess the company's long-term sustainability with regard to its ability to meet all its operational obligations. Let us see these ratios:

1. **Interest Coverage Ratio.** This ratio is also called the Debt Service Ratio or the Debt Service Coverage Ratio. It is used to measure a company's strength in repaying its liability towards interest on loans taken by the company. Higher this ratio, better it is. A number less than one, should raise alarm bells.

Interest Coverage Ratio = (Earnings Before Interest & Taxes / Interest Payment)

Knowing that Earnings Before Interest & Taxes (EBIT) = [EBITDA - (Depreciation & Amortisation Costs)], and EBITDA = (Revenue - Expenses) we can easily calculate Interest Coverage Ratio which is expressed as a multiple suggesting that for every Re of interest payment due, the company generates that many times its EBIT.

In the case of Exide Industries, EBITDA = Rs 1,737.01 crores as calculated earlier, EBIT = (1737.01-362.63) = Rs 1,374.38 crores, Finance Cost = Rs 9.40 crores, then

Interest Coverage = 1374.38 / 9.4 = 146.21 times. This means that for every rupee of interest due the company is generating an EBIT of 146.21

times. It may also mean that the company is not borrowing enough for investing in new products or technologies.

2. **Debt to Equity Ratio.** This ratio indicates the company's capability in fulfilling its liability obligations to its creditors. When this ratio is equal to 1, it means that the total debt and equity are equal, a number higher than 1 is a warning signal as it means that the company is highly leveraged. Prefer to invest in companies that have this ratio less than one.

Debt to Equity Ratio = (Total Debt / Total Equity)

In the case of Exide Industries, Total Debt − Long Term Debt + Short Term Debt = (2.95+275.41) = Rs 278.36 crores, and Total Equity = Rs 6,296.11 crores, then

Debt to Equity Ratio = 278.36 / 6296.11 = 0.04

3. **Debt to Asset Ratio.** This ratio helps in understanding the asset financing pattern of a company. It tells us how much of the company's assets are financed by debt.

Debt to Asset Ratio = (Total Debt / Total Assets) expressed as a percentage

In the case of Exide Industries, Total Debt = Rs 278.36 crores, Total Assets = Rs 8,242.08 crores, then

Debt to Asset Ratio = 278.36 / 8242.08 = 0.03 or 3%. This means that only 3% of the total assets are financed through debt.

4. **Financial Leverage Ratio.** The Financial Leverage Ratio helps in understanding to what extent are the company's assets supported by equity.

Financial Leverage Ratio = (Average Total Assets / Average Total Equity)

In the case of Exide Industries, Average Total Assets = Rs 8,207.25 crores and Average Total Equity = (6296.11 + 5986.99) / 2 = Rs 6,141.55 crores, then

Financial Leverage Ratio = 8207.25 / 6141.55 = 1.34. This means that the company supports 1.34 units of assets for each unit of equity.

A high number indicates greater leverage.

Operational Ratios

Operational Ratios are also referred to as Activity, Management or Asset Management Ratios. These ratios help us understand the efficiency of a company's operations. These ratios are:

1. **Fixed Assets Turnover Ratio.** This ratio is an indication of how efficiently the company is using its plant and machinery. Higher this ratio, better is the company. It is mostly used by capital intensive industries.

Fixed Assets Turnover Ratio = (Operating Revenues / Total Average Assets)

In the case of Exide Industries, Operating Revenues = Operating Revenues = Rs 9,856.66 crores, Total Average Assets = Rs 6,141.55 crores, then

Fixed Assets Turnover Ratio = 9856.66 / 6141.55 = 1.60

2. **Working Capital Turnover Ratio.** This ratio indicates how much revenue a company generates for every unit of working capital. Higher this ratio is for a company, the better it is.

Before calculating the Working Capital Turnover Ratio, we need to understand working capital.

Working Capital = (Current Assets - Current Liabilities)

If current assets are more than current liabilities, it means that the company has a surplus of working capital. When current liabilities are more than current assets, then the company is short of working capital.

Working Capital Turnover Ratio = (Revenue from Operations / Average Working Capital) expressed as a multiple

In the case of Exide Industries, Revenue from Operations = Rs 9,856.66 crores, Working Capital for 2019-20 = (3339.50-1744.25) = Rs 1,595.25, Working Capital for 2018-19 = (3471.97-1958.08) = Rs 1,513.89, Average Working Capital = (1595.25 + 1513.89) / 2 = Rs 1,554.57 crores, then

Working Capital Turnover Ratio = 9856.66 / 1554.57 = 6.34 times. This number indicates that for every rupee the company spends from the working capital, it generates an operational revenue of 6.34. A higher number means that the company's sales are better while utilising its working capital.

3. **Total Assets Turnover Ratio.** This ratio indicates the company's ability to generate revenues with the available assets. Higher the ratio, better is the company.

Total Assets Turnover Ratio = (Operating Revenue / Average Total Assets expressed as a multiple

For Exide Industries, Operating Revenue = Rs 9,856.66 crores, Average Total Assets = (8242.08+8172.42)/2 = Rs 8,207.25 crores, then

Total Assets Turnover Ratio = 9856.66 / 8207.25 = 1.20. Higher this number, better for the company.

4. **Inventory Turnover Ratio.** A company should be able to sell its inventory as quickly as possible. This ratio is used to check how quickly and efficiently it sells its products. This ratio should be compared between similar companies to understand how good or bad this number is.

Inventory Turnover Ratio = (Cost of Goods Sold / Average Inventory)

For Exide Industries, Cost of Goods Sold = Cost of materials consumed + Purchase of stock in trade + Stores and spare parts consumed + Power and fuel = (6519.80 + 6.17 + 68.24 + 331.59) = Rs 6,925.80 crores, Average Inventory = (2192.27 + 1803.97) = Rs 1,998.12 crores, then

Inventory Turnover Ratio = 6925.80 / 1998.12 = 3.47, This means that the company turnover its inventory about 3 times a year.

5. **Inventory Number of Days.** This number indicates how many days a company takes to convert its inventory to cash. Lower this number is, better for the company.

Inventory Number of Days = (365 / Inventory Turnover)

In the case of Exide Industries, Inventory Turnover = 3.47 as calculated above, then

Inventory Number of days = 365 / 3.47 = 105.19 days which means that the company is taking 105 days to convert its inventory to cash.

However, remember that a company with a higher inventory turnover ratio and a low inventory number of days may not always reflect that a company is great. This can happen when there are some production related issues. Therefore, it is important to read through the Management's Discussion & Analysis given in the annual report.

6. **Receivable Turnover Ratio.** This ratio indicates that how many times in a given period the company receives cash from its debtors and customers. Lower the ratio, better is the company.

Receivable Turnover Ratio = (Revenue / Average Trade Receivables) expressed as a multiple

In the case of Exide Industries, Revenue = Rs 9,856.66 crores, Average Trade Receivables = (815.30 + 1081.04) / 2 = Rs 948.17 crores, then

Receivables Turnover ratio = 9856.66 / 948.17 = 10.40 which means that the company receives payments about 10 times in a year.

7. **Days Sales Outstanding (DSO).** This ratio is also called as Average Collection Period or Day Sales in Receivables. This is used to check how quickly and efficiently the company collects its dues. Lower value indicates that the company is collecting its dues efficiently.

Average Collection Period = (365 / Receivables Turnover Ratio)

For Exide Industries, Receivables Turnover Ratio = 10.40 as calculated above, then

Days Sales Outstanding = 365 / 10.40 = 35.09 which means that the company receives money in about 35 days after it raises a sales invoice.

Valuation Ratios

Valuation Ratios help us in analysing whether the current price of the company's stock price is high or low. These ratios are:

1. **Price to Earnings Ratio (P/E).** This ratio helps you understand what an investor is willing to pay for each rupee a company earns. This ratio can

be found out by dividing current price of a share by the earnings per share. The current price of a stock is easily available through various websites. Earnings per share can be found from the financial statements of the company. A higher P/E is an indication that the company is overvalued and vice versa. However, a company may have a high P/E if its earnings are in line with projected earnings.

P/E Ratio = Market Price per Share / Earnings per Share

In case of Exide Industries, Market Price per Share as on 19 Feb 2021 = Rs 204.35, Earning per Share = Rs 9.71, then

P/E Ratio = 204.35 / 9.71 = 21.05 which means that for every unit of profit generated by the company, a buyer of its share is willing to pay Rs 21.05.

Avoid buying stocks that are trading at a P/E ratio of more than 30, no matter in which sector the company belongs to. The Earnings per Share can be easily manipulated by companies by changing their accounting policy too often or provisioning lower depreciation and thereby boosting earnings. Sometimes, you will notice that the company's earnings are increasing without an increase in cash flows and sales. When you see this, you need to be careful as something is clearly not all right.

2. **Price to Book Ratio (P/B).** This ratio is used to understand a company's value if it is sold today. Book value reflects a company's net worth. If this ratio is less than 1, investors assume that the company's assets are overvalued, and, if the ratio is too high investors feel that the assets are undervalued. Lower the value, better the company to invest in.

P/B Ratio = (Market Price per Share / Book Value per Share)

Book Value per Share = (Total Assets – Total Liabilities) / Total Number of Shares

The P/B Ratio is expressed as a multiple of its book value.

For Exide Industries, Book Value per Share = [6296.11-1744.25] / 85 = Rs 53.35

P/B Ratio = 204.35 / 53.35 = 3.83 which means that the company is trading 3.83 times its book value.

3. **Price to Sales Ratio (P/S).** Many investors prefer to use this ratio rather than the P/E ratio as earnings ratio may not give a true picture at all times especially in cyclical companies.

P/S Ratio = (Current Share Price / Sales per Share)
Sales per Share = (Total Revenue / Total Number of Shares)

The P/S Ratio is expressed as the number of times the stock is valued. Therefore, lower values of this ratio are considered as cheap stocks, and higher values as expensive stocks.

For Exide Industries, Total Revenue = Rs 9,856.66 crores, Total Number of Shares = 85 crores, then

Sales per Share = 9856.66 / 85 = 115.96

P/S Ratio = 204.35 / 115.96 = 1.76 which means that for every rupee of sale the stock is valued 1.76 times higher.

When comparing P/S ratio of two companies remember to check their profit margins also. The company with a higher profit margin retains a higher profit and therefore justifies a higher P/S ratio.

It is important to understand that all the ratios discussed above must be compared between similar companies and analysing their behaviour over a period of three to five years will lead to better evaluation and understanding their relevance.

There are several other ratios that you can use. Some of them are:

1. **Price to Earnings Growth Ratio (PEG).** This ratio is calculated by dividing its P/E by year over year growth rate of its earnings. Lower the value better is the company. Expected growth rate of a company can be found from websites of analysts who tracks that stock. A PEG ratio of 1 indicates perfect correlation between the current price and its projected earnings growth. If this ratio is greater than 1, then it means that the company is overvalued, and vice versa.

PEG Ratio = PE Ratio / Projected Annual Growth in Earnings

2. **EV/EBITDA Ratio.** This is a useful ratio to evaluate companies that carry heavy debts. A good company will have a lower value.

Enterprise Value (EV) = (Market Capitalisation + Debt – Cash), and EBITDA is Earnings Before Interest Tax Depreciation Amortisation.

3. **Earnings per Share (EPS).** This ratio is used to understand a company's profitability. A company that shows increase in EPS over a period is a good profitable company.

EPS = (Net Income - Dividends) / Average Outstanding Shares

4. **Free Cash Flow.** A higher value suggests that the company is generating more cash than it needs for its growth.

FCF = (Net Income + Non-Cash Expenses like depreciation and amortisation + Change in Working Capital) - Capital Expenses

5. **Cash Holding Per Share.** This is a valuation indicator that shows a company's strength. A strong company will show high amount of cash.

Cash Holding Per Share = Total Cash and Cash Equivalents / Number of Outstanding Shares

6. **Net Profit Margin.** A company that is good in converting revenue into more profits for shareholders is a company that is more desirable for investment.

Net Profit Margin = Net Income / Sales

7. **Dividend Yield.** This is profit that a company shares with its shareholders. Well established large companies give more dividends as their growth is saturated, and smaller growing companies may be paying lower dividends as they keep profits with them for expansion.

Dividend Yield = Dividend per Share / Price per Share

8. **Dividend Payout.** This will tell you what percentage of profits the company has paid as dividend. This is important for dividend seeking investors.

Dividend Payout = Dividend / Net Income

9. **Return on Net-worth.** This shows how much net profit a company has generated on shareholders money.

Return on Net Worth = Profit After Tax / Net Worth

10. **Current Ratio.** Current ratio indicates a company's strength in paying short term liabilities with short term assets. Prefer companies with a ratio of more than one.

Current Ratio = Current Assets / Current Liabilities

11. **Quick Ratio.** Quick ratio takes into account assets that can pay short term debts. This ratio is also called Acid Test Ratio. Prefer companies having this ratio greater than one.

Quick Ratio = (Current Assets - Inventory) / Current Liabilities

All these ratios can be easily calculated from the data that is available in the Annual Reports of companies. You don't have to calculate many of the important ratios as these can be found in various websites like value research online, money control, screener, etc.

Index Valuation

The valuation of indices like the Sensex and CNX Nifty 50 are measured by P/E, P/B and Dividend Yield ratios. The BSE & NSE publish these ratios on a daily basis by 1800 hours. Tracking an Index P/E ratio gives an investor an idea about how cheap or expensive the market is trading at any day.

Normally the Indian indices P/E ratio trades between 16x to 20x, with an average of 18x. The best time to invest is when the markets are trading below the average index P/E ratio.

When the index P/E valuation becomes too high, one can assume a correction is imminent.

10 CALCULATING INTRINSIC VALUE OF A STOCK

"Rich people make money when the stock market goes up, rich people make even more money when the stock market goes down"

Unknown

The quantum of profitability in an investment made in a stock market depends on which stock you buy, at what price you buy the stock and at what price you sell it.

So far, we have learnt how to pick the right stock. Now we need to buy it at the right price. Therefore, it is important to learn how a stock's right price can be derived. There are several ways of doing this, but we will use the most commonly used method, the Discounted Cash Flow (DCF) method, to find the intrinsic value of a stock. The intrinsic value of a stock is the price a rational investor is willing to pay while buying the stock.

The DCF model is made up of a few concepts which we must first understand for it is these very concepts that we will use in determining the intrinsic value of the stock we wish to buy:

1. **Future Cash Flow.** This concept can be best understood through an example. Let us say that you receive a proposal from a person selling a printing machine that costs Rs X which will give you a return of Rs 1,00,000 each year for the next 10 years. The residual value of the printing machine after 10 years may be assumed to be nil. But before you decide to get into this venture, you have an option to invest your money in a fixed deposit

which can give you a risk-free return of say 6%.

Let us say you decide to buy the printing machine. Since you have not opted for the fixed deposit you have foregone an opportunity to earn risk free interest of 6%. This is called Opportunity Cost that you will have to bear for buying the printing machine.

Since you will be getting regular cash flow of Rs 1,00,000 each year, therefore, the next question is to determine the value of each year's cash flow in today's terms. The answer to this question can be understood by the next concept, Time Value of Money.

2. **Time Value of Money.** The value of money is never constant, it keeps changing with time. When we make investments over a period of time, we wish to know, what would be the value of my investment in today's term, when it matures. This is called the Future Value. Conversely, if we have to find the value of an investment after a period of time in today's term, it is called Present Value.

In both the cases, we have to adjust the Opportunity Cost. This adjustment is called Compounding if we have to find the Future Value of money, and it is called Discounting when calculating Present Value.

Let us say that you wish to find the value of Rs 1,00,000 after 3 years assuming an opportunity cost of 6%. Using the following formula:

Future Value = Amount * (1 + Opportunity Cost Rate) ^ Number of Years

$$= 100000*[1+6/100)] \wedge 3$$

$$= 100000*[1.06*1.06*1.06]$$

$$= 100000*1.191$$

$$= 1,19,100.$$

In case we wish to know the present value of Rs 1,00,000 that is receivable after 4 years assuming an opportunity cost of 6%. Using the formula:

Present Value = Amount / (1+Discount Rate) ^ Number of Years

$$= 100000 \ / \ [1+(6/100)] \ ^ \wedge \ 4$$

$$= 100000 \ / \ [1.06*1.06*1.06*1.06]$$

$$= 100000 \ / \ 1.26246$$

$$= 79{,}210.43.$$

Having understood the concept of Time Value of Money, let us apply this model to understand how much you should pay to buy the printing machine. For this we need to evaluate the net Present value of Cash Flows.

3. **Net Present Value of Cash Flows.** In the example of the printing machine, we assumed that you would receive Rs 1,00,000 every year (say from 2021 onwards) for the next 10 years with an opportunity cost of 6%. Based on this we can tabulate the Present Value for each year.

Year	Cash Flow	Receivable in Year	Present Value
2021	1,00,000	1	94,340
2022	1,00,000	2	89,000
2023	1,00,000	3	83,962
2024	1,00,000	4	79,209
2025	1,00,000	5	74,726
2026	1,00,000	6	70,496
2027	1,00,000	7	66,506
2028	1,00,000	8	62,741
2029	1,00,000	9	59,190
2030	1,00,000	10	55,839

TOTAL	10,00,000		7,36,009

Table 7

The sum of all the present values of the future cash flows is called the Net Present Value, and this or less than this amount you should be willing to pay for buying the printing machine. In this case, you should not pay more than Rs 7,36,009 while buying the printing machine.

You would have noticed that the Present Value or the Future Value depend on two parameters, time and Opportunity Cost Rate. Therefore, both the assumptions should be made carefully and conservatively.

Now that we have understood the DCF model, we will replicate the same to determine the intrinsic value of a stock we wish to buy.

Finding the Intrinsic Value of a Stock

There are a few steps required to calculate the intrinsic value of a stock. Let us proceed methodically:

Step 1: Calculating Free Cash Flow (FCF)

Free cash is cash with the company is left with after paying all its expenses including investments. A healthy company will always have free cash. As investors we should always look for companies that have increasing free cash. FCF can be easily calculated by analysing the Cash Flow statement of the company.

FCF = (Cash from Operating Activities - Capital Expenditure)

From the Statement of Cash Flows of Exide Industries, we will calculate the FCF based on the historical FCF for the last three years as this is the most appropriate way of predicting the future FCF:

Particular	2017-2018	2018-19	2019-20
Net cash from operating activities	516.61	1003.79	913.63
Capital expenditures	772.17	676.08	465.98

Free Cash Flow (FCF)	(255.56)	327.71	447.65

Table 8

From the above table, the average FCF = (327.71+447.65-255.56)/3 = Rs 173.26 crores as all the figures in the table are in crores. Going ahead, we have to predict future growth rate of the company. It is important to be as conservative as possible while predicting growth rates. The growth potential in Large Cap companies is less than in Mid Cap companies, and the potential in Mid Cap companies is less than in Small Cap companies.

A company is considered as Large, Mid or Small Cap based on its market capitalisation. If the market capitalisation of a company is more than Rs 20,000 crores it is called a Large Cap, if it is between Rs 5,000 crores and less than Rs 20,000 crores it is a Mid Cap company, and if it is less than Rs 5,000 crores it is called a Small Cap.

As Exide is a midcap company with a market capitalisation of about Rs 16,889 crores and it has the potential to become a large cap company, it may be safe to assume a growth rate of 18% for the first 5 years and 10% for the next 5 years. For Large Cap companies, you can assume a growth rate of 15% for the first 5 years and then 10% for the next 5 years.

Based on the average FCF of Rs 173.26 crores for the year 2019-20, you can estimate the cash flows going forward with a growth rate of 18% for the first 5 years and thereafter with 10%.

FCF for 2020-21 = 173.26*(1+18%) = 173.26*1.18 = Rs 204.45 crores.

FCF for 2021-22 = 204.45*(1+18%) = 204.45*1.18 = Rs 241.25 crores.

In this way, going forward, you can estimate FCF for remaining years and tabulate them as under:

S No	Year	Assumed Growth Rate	FCF (in INR crores)
1	2020-21	18%	204.45
2	2021-22	18%	241.25

S No	Year	Assumed Growth Rate	FCF (in INR crores)
3	2022-23	18%	284.67
4	2023-24	18%	335.91
5	2024-25	18%	396.38
6	2025-26	10%	436.01
7	2026-27	10%	479.62
8	2027-28	10%	527.58
9	2028-29	10%	580.34
10	2029-30	10%	638.37

Table 9

Step 2: Calculating Terminal Value

You would have noticed that we have calculated FCF for 10 years, but companies continue to exist beyond 10 years, but the growth rate of free cash begins to diminish. This diminishing growth rate is called Terminal Growth Rate which is usually assumed to be less than 5%.

The sum of all the future free cash flows beyond the 10th year is called its Terminal Value. Since the time period is taken as infinity, the formula is:

Terminal Value = FCF * (1 + Terminal Growth Rate) / (Discount Rate - Terminal Growth Rate)

In our case of Exide Industries, FCF = Rs 638.37 crores; Terminal Growth Rate is assumed at 4%; Discount Rate assumed at 9%, then

Terminal Value = 638.37*(1+4%) / (9%-4%)

= [638.37*1.04] / (0.05)

$$= 663.90/0.05$$

$$= \text{Rs } 13{,}278 \text{ crores}$$

Step 3: Calculating Net Present Value

In this we need to find the value of all the cash flows in today's terms and their sum will be the Net Present Value.

For the year 2020-21, the FCF value we calculated was Rs 204.45 crores. Assuming a discount rate of 9% the present value would be:

Present Value = Amount / (1 + Discount Rate) ^ Number of Years

$$= 204.45 / (1+9\%) * 1$$

$$= 204.45/1.09$$

$$= \text{Rs } 187.59 \text{ crores.}$$

Similarly, we can find the Present Values of all the years and tabulate as under:

S No	Year	Growth Rate	FCF	Present Value
1	2020-21	18%	204.45	187.57
2	2021-22	18%	241.25	203.06
3	2022-23	18%	284.67	219.82
4	2023-24	18%	335.91	237.97
5	2024-25	18%	396.38	257.62
6	2025-26	10%	436.01	259.98
7	2026-27	10%	479.62	262.37
8	2027-28	10%	527.58	264.77

9	2028-29	10%	580.34	267.20
10	2029-30	10%	638.37	269.65
				2,430.01

Table 10

The total of all FCF as calculated above is Rs 2,430.01 crores. To this you need to add the Present Value of Terminal Value which is:

Present Value = Amount / (1 + Discount Rate) ^ Number of Years

$$= 13278 / (1+9\%) \wedge 10$$

$$= 13278 / (1.09) \wedge 10$$

$$= Rs\ 5608.77\ crores.$$

So, the Net Present Value = 2430.01+5608.77

$$= Rs\ 8,038.78\ crores.$$

Step 4: Calculating Share Price

You have calculated the Net Present Value of all free cash flows and this would be available to all shareholders of the company. You can now find the Share Price of Exide Industries. But before doing this, you need to determine the net debt that the company has. This can be found by looking into the current year's Balance Sheet.

Net Debt = Current Year Total Debt - Cash & Cash Balance

$$= 4.36 - 87.19$$

$$= Rs\ (82.83)\ crores.$$

A negative Net Debt number indicates that the company has more cash than debt which is a good sign. The Net Debt Value has to be added to the Net Present Value.

Total Present Value of all free cash flows = 8038.78 - (82.83) = Rs

8121.61 crores.

The formula for obtaining intrinsic value of a stock is:

Share Price (Intrinsic Value) = Total Present Value of all Free Cash Flows / Total Number of Shares

$$= 8121.61 \text{ crores}/85 \text{ crores}$$

$$= \text{Rs } 95.54.$$

Step 5: Calculating Intrinsic Value Band

To eliminate any errors that may have come up while determining the Intrinsic Value of the stock because of a few assumptions that were made, it is better to create an Intrinsic Value Band by increasing and decreasing it by 10%.

So, Intrinsic Value Band for Exide Industries Share = Rs 85.98 to Rs 105.09.

This means that the stock is fairly priced if it is available between Rs 85.98 to Rs 105.09.

Step 6: Interpretation of Intrinsic Value Band

1. When the stock is trading below Rs 85.98, it is considered as undervalued and, therefore, the best time to buy it.

2. When the stock is trading between Rs 85.98 to Rs 105.09, that is at its fair value, it is time to hold the stock and buying some more can be considered.

3. When the stock trades above Rs 105.09, it is considered as overpriced and, therefore you should avoid buying the stock. You can consider selling the stock or continue to hold.

The stock is trading at about Rs 198 as on 28 Jan 21 which is far above its fair value upper band of Rs 105.09.

Buying opportunities come during bear phases in a market when shares trade below their intrinsic value band. But such opportunities don't come every day, but when they come you should grab it with both hands.

11 PICKING WINNING STOCKS FOR INVESTING

"A lot of people with high IQs are terrible investors because they've got terrible temperaments. You need to keep raw, irrational emotion under control"

Charlie Munger

In the last few chapters, we have learnt how to carry out Financial Analysis of a stock. There are nearly 5,000 companies that are listed on the Bombay Stock Exchange and about 1,600 on the National Stock Exchange, most being listed on both the exchanges. It is impossible for individual investors to analyse all the companies due to understandable constraints in terms of effort and resources. Therefore, we need to develop a mechanism to short list a few stocks that we wish to analyse and then invest in. In this chapter, we will see how to pick the right stocks, firstly for analysing, and then investing in them by following a few steps:

Step 1

The first step should be to decide on what type of stocks you wish to buy in your portfolio. People with a low risk profile may be happy to buy stocks of bluechip companies. Others may choose companies that declare good dividends. Generally, people with a higher risk profile prefer to look for growth-oriented companies as these stocks generate better returns. However, it is prudent to have a diversified portfolio in terms of risk, sector and capital allocation.

Step 2

The second step should be to identify the sectors that are currently trending and in which you wish to invest in. This will easily come to you if you understand the macro economic trends and if you have kept yourself well informed by reading financial news and opinions.

Step 3

A sector will have several companies, or a sector may have a sub sector. For example, if you find that automobile is a trending sector, you need to narrow down your choice as it has a few sub sectors like 2&3 wheelers, ancillaries, cars & jeeps, light & heavy commercial vehicles and tractors. Similarly, under finance you have sub sectors like private banks, public sector banks, housing and others. Once you list out the sectors or sub sectors that interest you, your job of selecting companies can begin. From here things get a little difficult.

Step 4

There are some simple ways of shortlisting stocks that you may like to analyse:

1. One way to select stocks is by what you observe around you. For example, while travelling on roads, you notice that you see more cars or two wheelers of particular brands, or while you visit a mall for shopping you may notice that some shops or eatery brands attract more customers than others, you know which stock to short list.

2. The other simple way is to short list companies that are similar to the ones you work for. For example, if you work in a telecom company or a bank, you would be in a better position to evaluate such companies that fall under these sectors

3. Another way to short list stocks is by using a stock screener website. To do this, you need to decide on a few parameters that your stock should meet. For example, you can choose to short list stocks that have an ROE and PAT more than 25% and 20% respectively or companies that have no debt. You can choose any of the financial ratios that we studied. There are several websites that offer their basic service for free.

Step 5

The stocks that you may have short listed from serial 1 & 2 of Step 4, may not meet the criteria that you used while using the screener. However, if they are of any interest to you, you can keep them under a 'watch list' and analyse them when you notice that their business dynamics has changed over time. Try and choose companies that enjoy substantial competitive advantage over its competitors and avoid companies that are controlled or influenced by government policy.

Step 6

Once you are ready with your shortlisted companies, we begin analysing the companies based on the information posted on their respective websites and annual reports. You must first carry out a qualitative check of the companies to understand its management and business. There is no standard check list, but one can devise one so that you do not miss out any important point. Suggested check list is shown below:

S No	Question	Answer
1	What is the company's name?	
2	In which sector is the company?	
3	What does the company do?	
4	When was the company established?	
5	Where is the company's head office or corporate office located?	
6	How many plants or offices or outlets they have?	
7	Where are their plants or offices or outlets located?	
8	Are the plants running to full capacity?	

S No	Question	Answer
9	How many people work in this company?	
10	Are there any labour related issues affecting the company's performance?	
11	Is the company family run or managed by professionals?	
12	Who are the promoters of the company?	
13	What is the background of promoters?	
14	Has management's integrity ever been in doubt?	
15	Who are the board members?	
16	What percentage of shares are held by promoters?	
17	What products do they make?	
18	What services do they provide?	
19	Is any product or service a monopoly of the company?	
20	Which product or service generates maximum revenue?	
21	How many competitors does the company have?	
22	How difficult is it for a new company to enter into a similar business?	
23	Where do they sell their products or services?	

S No	Question	Answer
24	Who are their main customers?	
25	Do they sell their products or services outside India? If yes, where?	
26	What raw materials are required by them?	
27	Where do the raw materials come from?	
28	Do you see any bottlenecks in the supply of raw materials?	
29	How many subsidiaries does the company have?	
30	Does the company have plans for new products or services?	
31	What risks the company foresees to its business?	
32	Who are the company's bankers?	
33	Who are the company's auditors?	
34	Is the company controlled or managed by government?	
35	**FINAL ASSESSMENT**	**OK, CAN PROCEED WITH / NOT OK**

Table 11

If you find any issues with the qualitative analysis, especially with regard to management, it is best not to proceed further. However, if you are satisfied with the qualitative analysis results then only proceed to the next step.

Step 7

In this step we should list out the results of all relevant and important financial ratios after considering data for at least 5 years. All data to be collected from the company's annual reports. A check list could include the following:

S No	Check Point	Expectation	Result
1	Revenue Growth	Should have a CAGR of more than 15%	
2	PAT Growth	Should have a CAGR of more than 15%	
3	Gross Profit Margin	Should be more than 20%	
4	Net Profit	Should be in line with gross profit margin	
5	Earnings per Share (EPS)	Should be in line with net profits	
6	Debt / EBITDA Ratio	Should be decreasing over time	
7	Inventory Number of Days	Should be consistent and in line with PAT	
8	Sales & Receivables	Should show a decline	
9	Cash Flow from Operations	Should be positive and increase steadily	
10	Return on Equity (ROE)	Should be over 20%	
11	P/E Ratio	Should be less than 25	
12	Intrinsic Value of Stock	Around or lower than the stock's current market price	
13	FINAL RESULT	BUY / WAIT	

Table 12

The above check list has been prepared with Exide Industries in mind. It happens to be a manufacturing company. You may have to add or subtract a few check points depending on the industry that you choose.

12 CANDLESTICKS & CANDLESTICK CHARTS

"Markets are like women - always commanding, mysterious, volatile and unpredictable"

Rakesh Jhunjhunwala

Technical Analysis is used in identifying stocks that offer trading opportunities. Based on actions by market participants, patterns are formed when plotted on graphs. The interpretation of these patterns is made by the Technical Analysts.

In the last chapter, you studied how to use Fundamental Analysis in evaluating stocks. In this chapter you will learn Technical Analysis. Both are different approaches, as the former is used by investors and the latter by traders as well as investors. Difference is that investors remain invested for longer periods, whereas traders look for short term trading opportunities.

Trading in stocks is very risky when you trade without understanding.

Traders look for small and consistent profits as their stock holding period varies from a few minutes to a few weeks. As a trader you should be ready to book losses if a trade goes sour.

The biggest advantage of Technical Analysis is that its concept can be applied to any asset class unlike the Fundamental Analysis where the concepts change with respect to the commodity that is required to be analysed.

Technical Analyst pays no attention to the current price of a stock. He is interested only in how the stock price and the trade volumes move.

Technical Analysis is based on these assumptions:

1. All known and unknown information is reflected in the stock's price.

2. Once a trend, upward or downward, is established, the stock price moves accordingly.

3. Analysts believe that price history repeats itself. This happens because market participants react to price movements repeatedly in a similar manner. This is an extremely important assumption.

Types of Charts

During a day when shares are being traded, there are four important trade points to note. These are:

1. Opening Price (O)

2. Highest Price at which it traded (H)

3. Lowest Price at which it traded (L)

4. Closing Price (C)

There are three type of charts:

1. **Line Charts.** Line charts reflect only one price point, normally the closing price. These charts are simple and reflect a trend, but because they provide limited information they are not widely used.

2. **Bar Charts.** Unlike Line Charts, Bar Charts capture all four price points, OHLC. However, because they lack visual appeal, these are not used widely.

3. **Japanese Candlestick Charts.** These charts also capture all the four points, OHLC, and are widely used by analysts for their better visual appeal. Therefore, we shall see these in detail.

CANDLESTICKS

Bullish candles are usually represented in blue, green or white colour, and bearish candles in red or black. A candlestick is made up of three parts:

1. The central Real Body that connects the opening and closing price of a stock. A long Real Body depicts strong trading activity and large price movement, and a small Real Body depicts less trading activity with little price variation.

2. Upper Shadow that connects the high price to the closing price in bullish candles, and high price to open price in bearish candles.

3. Lower Shadow that connects the lowest price to the open price in bullish candles, and lowest price to closing price in bearish candles.

Bullish Candlestick

The different parts of a bullish candlestick are shown below:

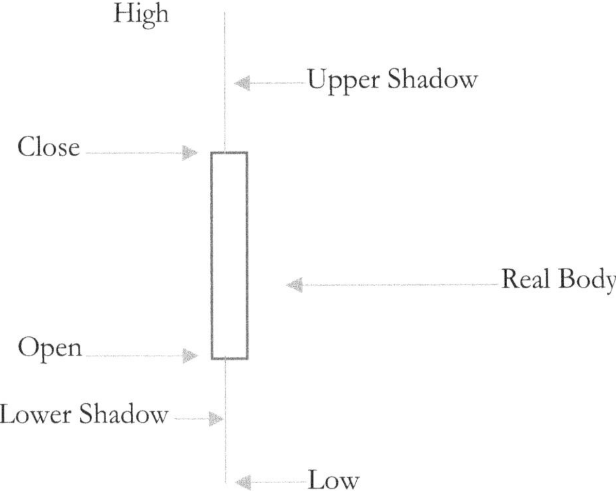

NOTE: To keep the cost of the book low, it is printed in black and white. Therefore, I am showing bullish candles as white and bearish candles as black which otherwise should be blue and red respectively. Usually on actual charts you will see them as blue and red.

As an example, if the prices for a particular stock on a day are: Open - 65, High - 80, Low - 60, Close - 75, these would be shown as:

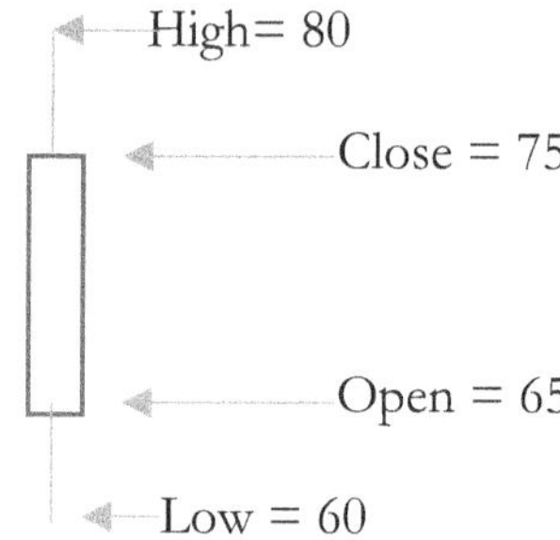

Bearish Candlestick

Different parts of a bearish candlestick are:

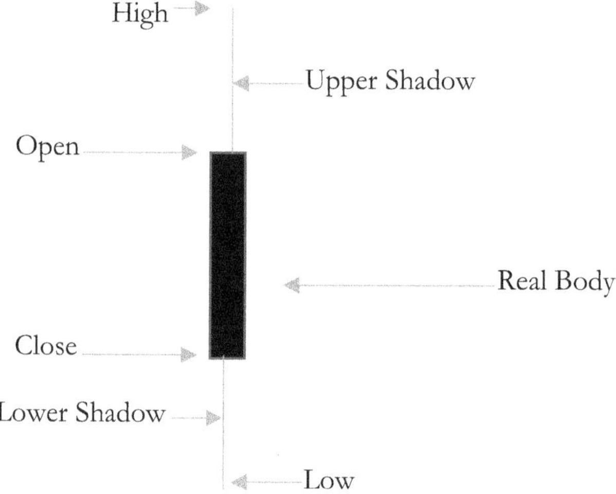

Note here the Open and Close points have been interchanged compared to a bullish candlestick.

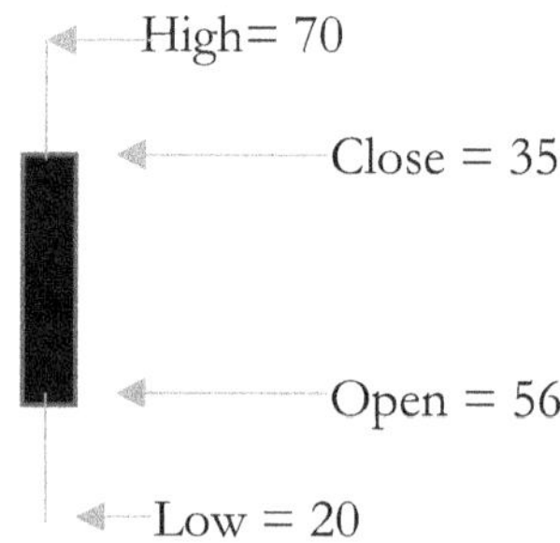

As an example, if the prices for a particular stock on a day are: Open -

56, High - 70, Low - 20, Close - 35, these would be shown as shown on last page.

A highly intense buying or selling activity is represented by Long Candlesticks, and activities that are low on intensity are represented by Short Candlesticks.

Time Frames

There are basically two parameters that a Technical Analyst studies, time frames and technical parameters. Some popularly used time frames on charts are:

1. Intraday Charts that could be 5 mins, 15 mins or 30 mins charts

2. Daily Charts

3. Weekly Charts

4. Monthly Charts

An investor can customise a time frame depending on which strategy he chooses to trade. Given below is what a candlestick will represent when viewed in different time frames:

Time Frame	Open	High	Low	Close	No of Candles
Monthly	Opening price as on first day of the month	Highest price during the entire month	Lowest price during the entire month	Closing price as on the last day of the month	12 candles for an entire year
Weekly	Monday's opening price	Highest price during the week	Lowest price during the week	Friday's closing price	52 candles for an entire year
Daily	Opening price for the day	Highest price during the day	Lowest price during the day	Closing price for the day	252 candles for an entire year

Time Frame	Open	High	Low	Close	No of Candles
Intraday 30 mins	Opening price at the 1st minute	Highest price during the 30 minutes duration	lowest price during the 30 minutes duration	Closing price at the 30th minute	12 candles per day
Intraday 15 mins	Opening price at the 1st minute	Highest price during the 15 minutes duration	lowest price during the 15 minutes duration	Closing price at the 15th minute	25 candles per day
Intraday 5 mins	Opening price at the 1st minute	Highest price during the 5 minutes duration	lowest price during the 5 minutes duration	Closing price at the 5th minute	75 candles per day

Table 13

Candlestick Patterns

Candlesticks are used to study patterns. There are two types of candlestick patterns:

1. **Single Candlestick Pattern.** Sometimes a single candlestick is enough to predict a trade. Under this we have:

a. Marubozu

b. Spinning Tops

c. Doji

d. Paper Umbrella

e. Shooting Star

2. **Multiple Candlestick Patterns.** These are patterns created with the help of two or three candlesticks. Under this we have:

a. Engulfing Pattern

b. Harami Pattern

c. Piercing Pattern

d. Dark Cloud Cover Pattern

e. Morning Star Pattern

f. Evening Star Pattern

Since these candlesticks were invented in Japan, their Japanese names still continue.

Single Candlestick Pattern: Marubozu

In Japanese, Marubozu means bald, and a Marubozu candlestick, by definition, has no upper and lower shadows. They are of two types:

1. **Bullish Marubozu.** Since a Marubozu has no upper and lower shadows, it follows strictly that for a Bullish Marubozu: **High = Close & Open = Low.** However, in reality a little variation between the High and Close or Open and Low is permitted. A Bullish Marubozu looks like this:

Such a candlestick signifies a buying opportunity.

2. **Bearish Marubozu.** Here too since a Marubozu has no upper and lower shoulders, it follows strictly that for a Bearish Marubozu: **High = Open & Close = Low.** In this case also a little variation between the High and Open or Close and Low is permitted. A Bearish Marubozu looks like this:

Such a candlestick signifies a selling opportunity.

Single Candlestick Pattern: Spinning Tops

A Spinning Top has a small real body, and the upper and lower shadows are equal. A small real body signifies that Close and Open prices are quite close, and for this reason the colour of the candlestick is not important. The upper and lower shadows are equal, which means that neither the bulls nor the bears could influence the price movement in a direction. Therefore, we can conclude that Spinning Tops just convey indecision and are best analysed in conjunction with an already established upward or downward trend.

Spinning Tops look like this:

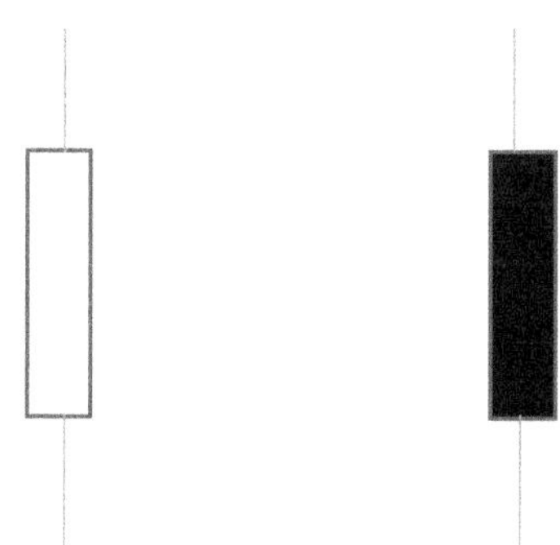

When a Spinning Top is seen during an upward or a downward trend, there are two possibilities, either the trend will continue, or it may change direction. A trader should be cautious before taking a call either way.

Single Candlestick Pattern: Doji

Dojis are similar to Spinning Tops as they also convey indecision. Strictly speaking, they should have no real body. However, candlesticks having wafer thin real bodies can also be considered as Dojis. As they have no real body, there is no or extremely low difference between Closing and Opening prices. The length of both shadows can be different. Dojis appear as shown below:

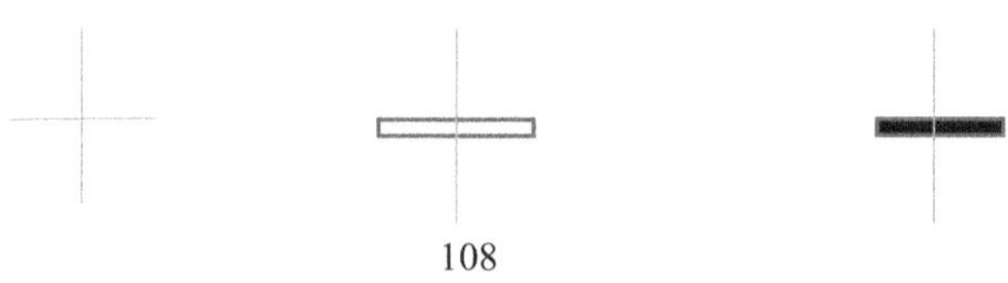

As the real body of a Doji is wafer thin, colour of the real body is of no significance. Spinning Tops and Dojis, generally are seen in clusters. As with Spinning Tops, a trader should be cautious in taking trading calls.

Single Candlestick Pattern: Paper Umbrella

When the lower shadow length a candlestick is more than twice the length of real body, that candlestick is called a Paper Umbrella.

For example, in a bullish candle, the Open = 30, Close = 33, High = 34 and Low = 40, then the body length works out to (33-30) = 3, and the length of lower shadow = (40-30) = 10 which is more than twice the length of the real body. Hence, such a candle will be called a Paper Umbrella. Paper Umbrellas look like this:

Paper Umbrellas indicate change in a trend depending on where it is found on a chart. The Paper Umbrella candlestick shows two reversal trends:

1. **Hammer.** If the Paper Umbrella is found at the end of a downward trend, it is called a Hammer.

2. **Hanging Man.** When a Paper Umbrella is seen at the end of an upward trend, it is called a Hanging Man.

Single Candlestick Pattern: Shooting Star

A Shooting Star is an inverted form of a Paper Umbrella. Here, the length of the upper shadow is more than twice the length of real body. Strictly, it should have no lower shadow but a small one may be permitted.

For example, in a bullish candle, the Open = 30, Close = 33, High = 44 and Low = 29, then the body length works out to (33-30) = 3, and the length of the upper shadow = (44-33) = 11which is more than twice the length of the real body. Hence, such a candle will be called a Shooting Star. Shooting Stars look like this:

A Shooting Star is indicative of a bearish pattern to follow. Hence, it is seen at the top end of an upward trend.

Multiple Candlestick Pattern: Engulfing Pattern

An Engulfing Pattern requires two candlesticks, a small candle on the first day and a longer one the next day that seems to be engulfing the first one. If such a pattern is seen at the bottom of a downward trend, it is called a Bullish Engulfing Pattern. On the other hand, if it is seen at the top of an upward trend, it is called a Bearish Engulfing Pattern.

Some analysts consider engulfing only the real body as sufficient, some say that the whole of the smaller candlestick should be engulfed to signal presence of an Engulfing Pattern.

Multiple Candlestick Pattern: Piercing Pattern

The Piercing Pattern is similar to the Bullish Engulfing Pattern. Here, the condition is that more than 50% but less than 100% of the bearish candle of the previous day should be engulfed by the bullish candle on the next day.

For example, if the Close Open range of a bearish candle on a previous day is 20, and the range next day of a bullish candle is 12 which is 60% of 20 and since it is more than 50% as also less than 100%, it is called a Piercing Pattern.

Multiple Candlestick Pattern: Dark Cloud Cover Pattern

This pattern is similar to a Bearish Engulfing Pattern. Here, the condition is that more than 50% but less than 100% of the bullish candle of the previous day should be engulfed by the bearish candle on the next day.

For example, if the Close Open range of a bullish candle in a previous day is 20, and the range of a bearish candle on the next day is 12 which is 60% of 20 and since it is more than 50% as also less than 100%, it is a Dark Cloud Cover Pattern.

Multiple Candlestick Pattern: Harami Pattern

Harami in Japanese means pregnant. This pattern is formed with the help of two candles, generally one bullish and the other bearish. The first candle is long and the second one is short. The appearance of a Harami signals a trend reversal. There are two types of Harami:

1. **Bullish Harami Pattern.** In this pattern, the first day's bearish candle is a long one and the bullish candle is a short one that appears at the end of a downward trend, signalling commencement of an upward trend.

2. **Bearish Harami Pattern.** In this pattern, the first day's bullish candle is a long one and the bearish candle is a short one that appears at the end of an upward trend, signalling commencement of a downward trend.

Multiple Candlestick Pattern: Morning Star Pattern

This pattern is formed with the help of three candles. The first day's candle would be a long bearish candlestick indicating a new low. On the second day, the stock would open with a gap down opening and ending the day with either a Doji or a Spinning Top candlestick. On the third day, the stock opens with a gap up opening and ends the day by recovering all losses of day one.

A Morning Star Pattern can be found at the bottom of a downward trend. Hence, a Morning Star signifies a bullish trend.

Multiple Candlestick Pattern: Evening Star Pattern

An Evening Star Pattern is the opposite of the Morning Star Pattern. This pattern signifies a bearish trend to follow, and such a pattern is found at the top of an upward trend. This pattern is also formed by three candles.

On the first day, the stock would open gap up, making new highs, thus forming a long bullish candlestick. On the second day, again the stock opens with a gap up but by the end of day leaves a Doji or Spinning Top candlestick. On the third day, the stock opens with a gap down, ending the day with a bearish candle, thus signalling commencement of a bearish trend.

Summary

Pattern	No of Candlesticks	Pattern Characteristics	Pattern Signal
Bullish Marubozu	1	No upper and lower shadows	Buying opportunity
Bearish Marubozu	1	No upper and lower shadows	Selling opportunity
Spinning Tops	1	Small real body, equal upper and lower shadows	Indecision
Doji	1	No or wafer-thin real body	Cautious
Paper Umbrella: Hammer or Hanging Man	1	Lower shadow length is more than twice the length of real body and no upper shadow	Change in trend
Shooting Star	1	Upper shadow length is more than twice the length of real body and no lower shadow	Bearish trend
Bullish Engulfing Pattern	2	A small bearish candle on first day and a longer bullish one the next day seen at the bottom of a downward trend	Upward trend
Bearish Engulfing Pattern	2	A small bullish candle on first day and a longer bearish one the next day seen at the top of an upward trend	Downward trend
Piercing Pattern	2	More than 50% but less than 100% of the first day bearish candle should be engulfed by the next day bullish candle	Upward trend

Pattern	No of Candlesticks	Pattern Characteristics	Pattern Signal
Dark Cloud Cover	2	More than 50% but less than 100% of the first day bullish candle should be engulfed by the next day bearish candle	Downward trend
Bullish Harami	2	First day's long bearish candle followed by next day's short bullish candle seen at the end of a downward trend	Upward trend
Bearish Harami	2	First day's long bullish candle followed by next day's short bearish candle seen at the end of an upward trend	Downward trend
Morning Star	3	Long bearish candle on first day, second day gap down opening and closing with a Doji or Spinning Top, gap up opening on third day recovering all losses of first day. This pattern is seen at the bottom of a downward trend	Upward trend
Evening Star	3	Long bullish candle on first day, second day gap up opening and closing with a Doji or Spinning Top, gap down opening on third day leaving a bearish candle. This pattern is seen at the top of an upward trend	Downward trend

Table 14

13 VOLUME, RESISTANCE & SUPPORT LEVELS

"The individual investor should act consistently as an investor and not as a speculator

Ben Graham

Volumes are another trend that a Technical Analyst keeps a watch on as it tells us how many shares have been bought and sold over a period of time. However, volume information on its own has little meaning but when analysed in conjunction with preceding volume and price trends, then volume information becomes meaningful.

When price and volume both show signs of increased activity, the expectation is that the price of the stock will rise further signalling a bullish trend.

When price increases but volumes decrease, a trader must get cautious as it signifies that weak hands are buying the stock.

When price and volume both decrease, again the trader should get cautious as it signifies that weak hands are selling the stock.

When price decreases and volume increases, the expectation is that the price will fall further, thereby signalling a bearish trend.

The volume of a particular day is compared with the last 10 days average volume. If the today's volume is more than the 10 days average volume it is then considered as High Volume, and if the today's volume is less than the

10 days average volume then it is considered as Low Volume.

Resistance & Support Levels

Resistance or Support Levels are the points identified on charts where the price of a stock or an index acts as a barrier to further growth or decline. Technical Analysts use this tool while analysing rising and falling markets. For the trader resistance signals selling and support signals buying.

Resistance is expected when there is a likelihood of excess supply which results in building selling pressure that tends to bring the price lower. On the other hand, Support is expected when there is a likelihood of dearth of supply which results in building buying pressure that in turn tends to make the price rise.

The Resistance Level is always greater than the current price of the stock or index, and the Support Level is always lower than the current price.

The way to determine Resistance and Support levels is the same. These levels are found by marking straight lines connecting a few similar data points on a chart. This can be done by following the method described below:

1. **Load Data Points.** For short term traders, it is enough to load 3 to 6 months data, whereas for long term investors 12 to 18 months data is enough.

2. **Identifying and Aligning Price Action Zones.** At least three price action zones should be identified for resistance and support levels separately. Price action zones are zones that display hesitation in up or down moves or sharp reversals. There could be several such zones, but it is best to determine at least three that are at the same level as also at least three to four weeks apart.

3. **Drawing Horizontal Lines.** Draw horizontal lines connecting the three price action zones that displayed hesitation in moving up or sharp downward reversal, and the three action zones that displayed hesitation in moving down or sharp upward reversal. The first line would be the Resistance Level and the second is the Support Level.

The Support and Resistance lines so drawn are only indicative of possible price reversals and be treated as such. There would be several instances where these levels would be broken, and fresh Resistance and Support levels would then be required to be determined.

To eliminate any possible errors, it is best to determine Support and Resistance levels in terms of a range. For example, if the horizontal line determines a price of say Rs 200 for a particular stock as its support level, then it would be better to describe the support level as between Rs 198 to Rs 202.

14 LAGGING & LEADING INDICATORS

"Stop trying to predict the direction of stock markets, the economy or the elections"

Warren Buffett

To analyse price movements, Technical Analysts use technical indicators. These indicators are used in addition to the study of candlestick charts, volumes, resistance and support lines. Indicators are of two types:

1. **Lagging Indicators.** Lagging indicators lag price which means that a reversal or a new trend is signalled after it has occurred. In spite of the signal occurring after the event, these are still very much useful.

2. **Leading Indicators.** Leading indicators lead price thereby predict occurrence of a reversal or a new trend in advance. However, a trader should be careful while using them as their accuracy is suspect. Most leading indicators are oscillators, that is, they oscillate within a range.

LAGGING INDICATORS

Some important lagging indicators are:

1. Moving Averages

2. MACD

3. Bollinger Bands

Types of Moving Averages

There are various types of moving averages, however, we shall discuss the following two which are important from our point of view:

1. Simple or Arithmetic Moving Averages

2. Exponential Moving Averages

Simple Moving Averages

If we were to calculate the average height of three children whose individual heights are 1.6m, 1.8m and 1.4m, we would add up all the three heights (1.6+1.8+1.4) and divide it by 3 to get the average height of 1.6m.

However, the concept of a moving average is a little different. Let us consider the closing price of a stock moved as under:

1 Jan 21	Rs 220
2 Jan 21	Rs 235
3 Jan 21	Rs 228

Average price movement for these three days is then (220+235+228)/3 = Rs 227.66

Now let us say that the closing price of the next three days after 1 Jan 21 are as under:

2 Jan 21	Rs 235
3 Jan 21	Rs 228
4 Jan 21	Rs 240

The average price movement for these three days is then (235+228+240) = Rs 234.33

Similarly, the next several average price movements can be calculated, and all these would be called Simple Moving Averages. What we are essentially doing is discarding the oldest data of each group and adding the data of the following new day. This can be easily done on an Excel Sheet.

Once we have calculated the moving averages, we can plot them on a graph that would appear as a smooth curving line called the Simple Moving Average Line. These moving lines can be drawn for any number of days, for example 5,10, 50, 100, 200 days and these can be overlaid on other graphs.

Exponential Moving Averages

While calculating Simple Moving Averages we gave equal weightage to all the data points. However, in the Exponential Moving Averages, each data point is given a weightage. A new data point gets more weightage as compared to the earlier data points. The average thus calculated based on weighted data points is called the Exponential Moving Average.

If you will plot the Simple and the Exponential Moving Average lines onto a candlestick chart, you will notice that the Exponential Moving Average line hugs the candles more than the Simple Moving Average line. This is why traders give more importance to Exponential Moving Averages than Simple ones.

Moving Average Lengths

The common moving average lengths are generally 10, 20, 50, 100 and 200 days. However, they can be created for any length of time. These can be plotted on any chart time frame an investor or trader chooses.

Shorter the length of the moving average, more quickly it will react to price changes. Shorter lengths are used by traders and longer lengths by long term investors.

Moving Average Crossover Strategies

Moving Averages can be usefully employed to predict buying and selling opportunities. When a stock price moves above the moving average line, it signifies a buying opportunity. On the other hand, when the stock price moves below the moving average line it is a selling opportunity.

Traders use a Combination of two or more moving average lines.

Typically, traders use a 50 and a 100 days moving averages. In this case, the 50 days moving average is the shorter moving average and also faster, and the 100 days moving average is the longer moving average and slower. When both these moving averages are plotted on a candlestick graph, you will notice that they criss-cross each other at a few points.

When the faster average line crosses and goes above the slower one, it indicates a bullish trend, and this trend lasts till the faster average line goes below the slower average line. So, the longer the time frames you choose fewer will be the trading opportunities that would be thrown up.

Moving Averages can be used on their own or can be the basis of other technical indicators.

Moving Averages Convergence & Divergence (MACD)

MACD can simply be explained as convergence and divergence of two moving averages. Convergence results when the two moving averages move closer to each other, and when they move away from one another it is called divergence.

A standard MACD is calculated with a 12 and 26 days exponential moving averages, considering closing price of each day. However, you can choose your own time frames.

Without going into the details of how MACD is calculates, it is sufficient to know that the MACD value is equal to (12 days EMA - 26 days EMA), and calculated like moving averages, then plotted and represented as a line that oscillates on either side of a central line as it will have negative and positive numbers.

A positive sign indicates a bullish trend in the stock's price, and a negative value indicates the opposite. The difference between the two moving averages is called the MACD spread. When spread starts to decrease it signifies commencement of reduction in momentum, and when spread starts to increase then it signifies that momentum will gain strength.

A 9-day simple moving average of the MACD is called the signal line. The MACD line and the signal line are used in conjunction for applying the crossover strategy. As the MACD is a trend following system, the crossover points signal a buy or sell trade.

Bollinger Bands

Bollinger Bands are used to identify oversold and overbought levels as they help a trader in deciding when to buy or sell.

Bollinger Bands consist of three parts:

1. The Middle Line that represents a 20-days simple moving average based on closing price.

2. The Upper Band that is +2 standard deviation of the middle line.

3. The Lower Band that is -2 standard deviation of the middle line.

Let us say, a stock's 20-days simple moving average is 8,000 and the standard deviation is 50, then with the +2 standard deviation the value of the 20-days simple average would be 8000+(50*2) = 8100, and with the -2 standard deviation it will be 8000-(50*2) = 7900. By our definition of Bollinger Bands, the middle line represents the average stock price, the price in the upper band will show that its price is more than the average, and the lower band indicates the price is below the average price. So, upper and lower bands signal selling or buying opportunity.

LEADING INDICATORS

Some of the important leading indicators are:

1. Relative Strength Index (RSI)

2. Stochastic Oscillator

3. Williams % R

Relative Strength Index (RSI)

RSI is used to identify trend reversals. The formula for calculating RSI is:

RSI = 100 - [100 / (1 + Relative Strength)], and Relative Strength = (Average Gain) / (Average Loss).

From the formula it can be seen that the value of RSI will oscillate in a range between 0 and 100. Therefore, it is also called a momentum oscillator. The default period for hourly charts is 14 hours and for daily charts it is 14 days. However, this is not sacrosanct, you can use a period you desire.

If the RSI value is between 0 and 30, then the stock is presumed to be oversold and its price is ready to move upward. If the RSI value is between 70 and 100, the stock is presumed to be overbought and its price is ready to move downward.

The interpretation may not always be what is stated above. If the RSI value of a stock remains in the oversold or overbought zones for prolonged periods, one can look for selling or buying opportunities respectively. If the RSI value starts to move out after a prolonged period in the oversold zone, it is a signal to buy, and if the RSI value starts to move out after a prolonged period in the overbought zone, then one can consider a selling opportunity.

Stochastic Oscillator

A Stochastic Oscillator is very much like the RSI we discussed above. However, the RSI is represented by a single line, the Stochastic Oscillator has two lines. One line represents the actual oscillator, and the other line represents the three-day simple moving average. Where the two intersect, it is a signal that there may be a large change in momentum coming.

The formula for calculating Stochastic Oscillator, %K is:

%K = [(C - L14) / (H14 - L14)] * 100, where C is the most recent closing price, L14 is the lowest traded price in the last 14-days period, H14 is the highest traded price in the last 14-days period.

This oscillator's values are between 0 and 100. The settings required for this indicator are:

%K Period is the current value of the Stochastic Oscillator, also called the faster oscillator.

%K Slowing is the difference between the fast and slow oscillators.

%D Period which is the value of (3 - period moving average of %K), also called the slower oscillator.

The interpretation of the Stochastic Oscillator and RSI are similar.

RSI tracks the overbought and oversold levels by measuring the velocity of price movements, whereas the Stochastic Oscillator assumes that closing prices should close near to the same direction as the current trend. Therefore, RSI is more useful in trending markets and Stochastic Oscillator is more useful when markets move sideways or when they are very choppy.

Williams %R

This is a momentum indicator that is inverse of the fast Stochastic Oscillator. This is represented by a single line. It oscillates between 0 and -100 and measures overbought and oversold levels.

The formula for calculating Williams %R is:

Williams %R = [(Highest High - Close) / (Highest High - Lowest Low)] * 100, where Highest High and Lowest Low correspond to the highest and lowest closing prices during the last 14-days period, and Close is the most recent closing price.

This indicator helps the trader understand where the current price is relative to the highest high during the last 14-days period. This 14-days period is not sacrosanct, use can choose any period. When the indicator is between 0 and -20, the stock is considered to be in the overbought zone, and when it is between -80 and -100 the stock is considered to be in the oversold zone.

On-Balance Volume (OBV)

This is a cumulative indicator that measures buying and selling pressure by adding volumes on up days and subtracting volumes on down days.

If the closing price is higher than the previous day's closing price, then

New OBV = Current OBV + Volume

If the closing price is lower than the previous day's closing price, then

New OBV = Current OBV - Volume

The direction of the OBV line is more important than the value of the OBV. A rising OBV line indicates increased demand which signals a buying opportunity, and a dropping OBV line indicates decreased demand which is a signal to sell.

15 FIBONACCI RETRACEMENTS & THE DOW THEORY

"One of the funny things about the stock market is that every time one person buys, another sells, and both think they are astute"

William Feather

The Fibonacci series consists of a sequence of numbers commencing from 0 such that the value of any number in the series is a sum of the previous two numbers. The series looks like this:

0, 1, 1, 2, 3, 5, 8, 13, 21, 34, 55, 89, 144, 233, 377, 610, 987…. to infinity

The series throws up some very interesting ratios:

1. If you divide any number in the series by its previous number, the ratio is approximately equal to 1.618:

987/610 = 1.618

377/233 = 1.618

This ratio is also called the Golden Ratio as it is found in human face, flowers, animal bodies, galaxy and rock formations, vegetables, etc and represented by phi.

2. If you divide any number in the series by its next number, the ratio is approximately equal to 0.618:

$233/377 = 0.618$

$89/144 = 0.618$

If 0.618 is expressed as a percentage, then it is equal to 61.8%

3. If you divide any number in the series by a number that is two places higher, the ratio is approximately equal to 0.382:

$21/55 = 0.382$

$89/233 = 0.382$

If 0.382 is expressed as a percentage, then it is equal to 38.2%

4. If you divide any number in the series by a number that is three places higher, the ratio is approximately equal to 0.236:

$34/144 = 0.236$

$21/89 = 0.236$

If 0.236 is expressed as a percentage, then it is equal to 23.6%

Technical Analysts believe that these ratios 23.6%, 38.2% and 61.8% can be used for Retracement Level to forecast whether the stock prices will move upwards or downwards. By using these retracement levels, you can predict a fall of 23.6% or 38.2% or 61.8% from the stock price peaks, thus enabling you to buy the stock. Similarly, you can predict the level to which a stock price can rise to after the fall is over, thus enabling the trader to take a sell call. You can construct Retracement Levels by following the simple steps as under:

Step 1. Identify two immediate high and low peaks. Note the price change and consider this to be equivalent to 100%.

Step 2. From the chart tools, select the Fibonacci Retracement Tool.

Step 3. To connect the high and low points you have selected, firstly click on the low point and drag the line to the high point. Once this is done, the software plots the Fibonacci Retracement levels automatically.

THE DOW THEORY

The Dow theory being more than a hundred old theory, and much has changed since then, the theory has admirers and critics. The theory is built on a few assumptions:

1. **Market Indices Discount Everything.** The market indices discount everything that is known or unknown in the public domain.

2. **Three Market Trends.** Stock markets consider three trends - primary, secondary and minor. A primary trend lasts from a year to a few years and are of interest to long term investors. A primary trend can be an upward or a downward trend. A secondary trend relates to corrections or pullbacks during a primary trend and may last from about three weeks to three months. Lastly, a minor trend lasts for less than three weeks that account for daily fluctuations and is also referred as noise.

3. **All Indices Must Confirm Trend.** A market trend can be classified as bullish or bearish when all indices confirm the same, that is, the Nifty, Mid Cap and Small Cap all move in the same direction.

4. **Volumes Must Confirm Trend.** Volumes confirm a trend. In a bull market the volume should increase as the price rises, and volumes reduce as the price falls. In a bear market, volumes increase as price falls, and volume decreases as price rises.

5. **Sideway Markets can Substitute Secondary Trends.** When markets trade within a range over an extended time, they are said to be Sideway. Sideway Markets can be a substitute for secondary market trends.

6. **Closing Price is Most Sacred.** Out of all the price levels, opening, high, low and closing, the closing price of the day is most important.

Three Phases of a Market

As per the Dow theory, a market has three distinct phases:

1. **Accumulation Phase.** This phase is after a steep fall in markets when the prices are rock bottom, market participants are fearful, and the low stock price languishes for a while. This is the time when long term institutional investors start buying stocks in large quantities over an

extended period of time.

2. **Mark up Phase.** Once the institutional investors are done with their accumulation of stocks, the traders start chipping in and the stock prices begin to rise sharply and quickly because of which many retail investors are left behind.

3. **Distribution Phase.** During this phase, several stocks break their 52 weeks high and everyone starts talking about the markets. The institutional investors who had bought beaten down stocks during the accumulation phase, notice the high profits they can make, start selling their stocks and the market eventually enters the bear phase. The accumulation phase begins again.

A word of caution here, is that no two cycles are similar. As investors or traders, you will have to judge the trends continuously while making buying and selling decisions.

Dow Patterns

There are several patterns in the Dow theory, and these can be classified under two heads, Continuation Patterns and Reversal Patterns:

Continuation Patterns

These patterns are formed when the market enters a consolidation or correction phase, and the indication is that this trend is likely to continue. Valid continuation patterns could be:

1. **Symmetrical Triangles.** These appear in an upward or a downward trend and characterised by a series of higher lows and lower highs.

This pattern will look like this:

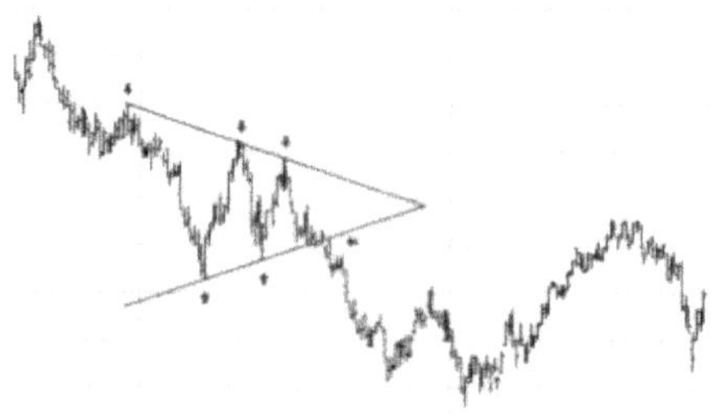

These symmetrical triangles indicate a period of indecision as forces of demand and supply are equal. The price projection is obtained by measuring the widest part of the triangle and then adding it to or subtracting it from the breakout point depending on the direction of existing trend.

2. **Ascending Triangle.** This pattern is similar to the symmetrical triangle pattern except that the top trend line is a horizontal resistance line.

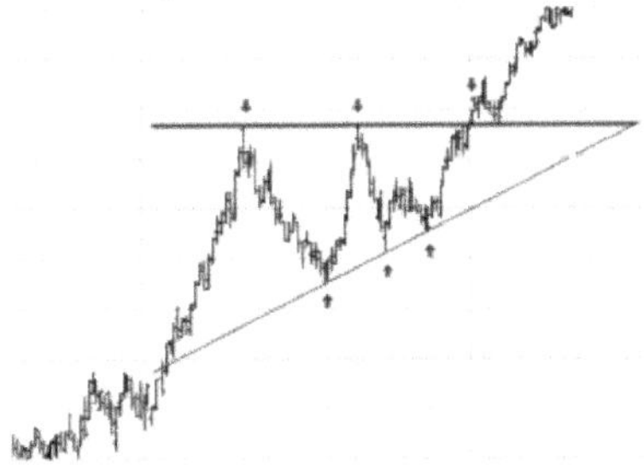

An entry signal to buy is given when the price breaks out of the horizontal resistance line that   should   occur   about   66%   inside   the triangle. If it breaks out near the apex, then it is not a valid entry signal. The price projection is obtained by measuring the widest part of the triangle and adding it to the breakout point.

3. **Descending Triangle.** This pattern is also similar to the symmetrical triangle pattern except that the lower trend line is a horizontal resistance line.

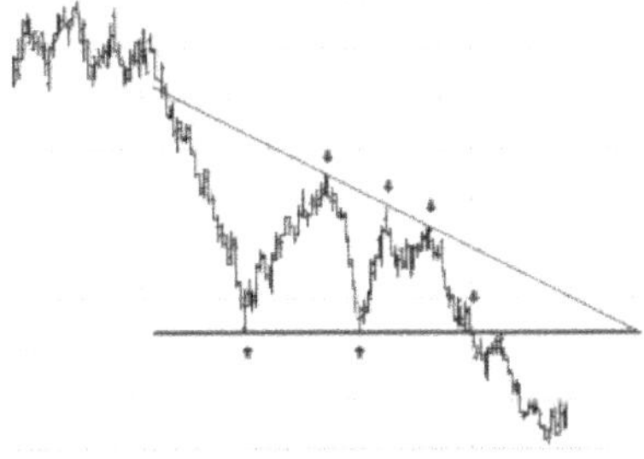

An entry signal to sell is given when the price breaks out of the horizontal resistance line that should occur about 66% inside the triangle. If it breaks out near the apex, then it is not a valid entry signal. The price projection can be obtained by measuring the widest part of the triangle and subtracting it from the breakout point.

4. **Rectangle Pattern.** This pattern is formed when the price moves between a support and a resistance line several times touching them every time.

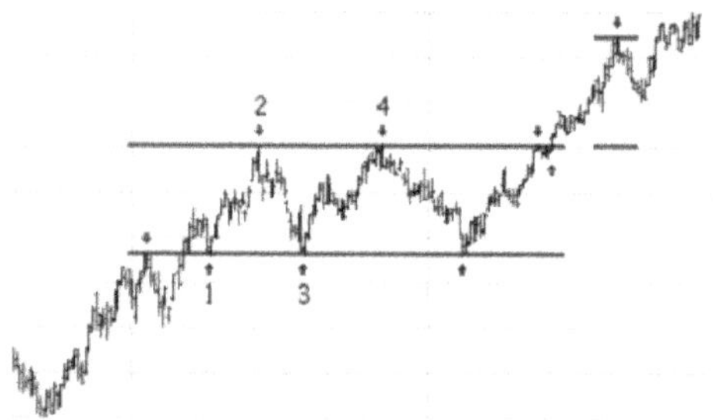

If the price breaks out of the upper line then it is a buy signal, and if it breaks out of the bottom line then it is a sell signal. The price projection can be measured by the height of the rectangle.

5. **Flag Pattern.** This pattern occurs when there is rapid and steep price rise followed by a short period of congestion or consolidation with low volumes.

In this pattern, the entry signal is given when the price breaks out of the parallelogram or rectangle formed during the congestion area of the flag. It is a buy signal if the breakout is in the direction of the flagpole. The price projection can be measured by measuring the flagpole length.

6. **Pennant Pattern.** This pattern is similar to the flag pattern except that instead of a parallelogram or rectangle a triangle is formed. The below figure shows a typical pennant pattern.

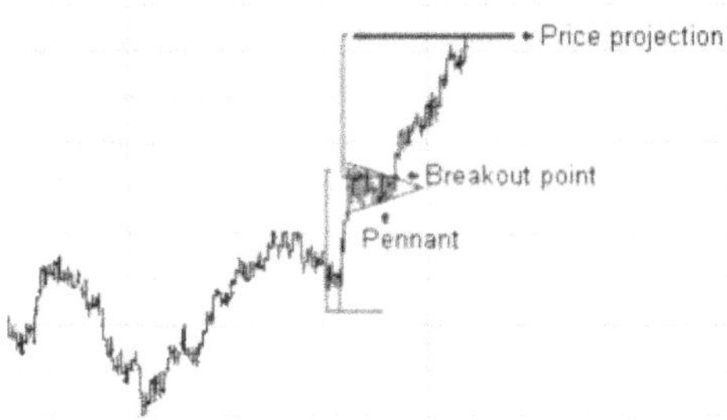

In this pattern, the entry signal is given when the price breaks out of the triangle formed during the congestion area. It is a buy signal if the breakout is in the direction of the preceding sharp increase. The price projection can be measured by the length of the sharp rise.

7. **Cup & Handle Pattern.** This pattern indicates a bullish trend. The pattern is made up of two parts, the cup and the handle.

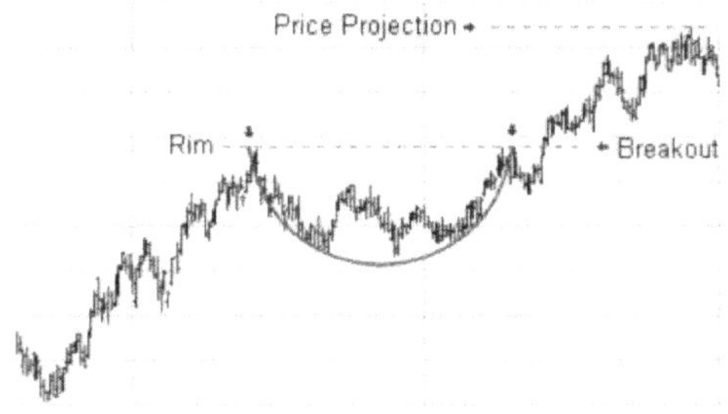

The cup is formed with a series of gentle declines in price after interrupting an upward trend. The handle is formed of a congested consolidation period after the cup is formed.

This pattern signals a buy when the price breaks out from the handle. The minimum price projection can be calculated by measuring the depth of the cup.

Reversal Patterns

These patterns indicate a high probability of a trend reversal. Like in continuation patterns, an existing trend should be there.

1. **Double Tops & Bottoms.** Double Tops pattern is a bearish reversal trend that often marks the end of an upward trend, whereas the Double Bottoms pattern is a bullish reversal trend. The Double Tops pattern

consists of two consecutive peaks at almost the same level, and the Double Bottoms pattern consists of two consecutive dips.

In this pattern, the entry signal is given when the price breaks out of the triangle formed during the congestion area. It is a buy signal if the breakout is in the direction of the preceding sharp increase. The price projection can be measured by the length of the sharp rise.

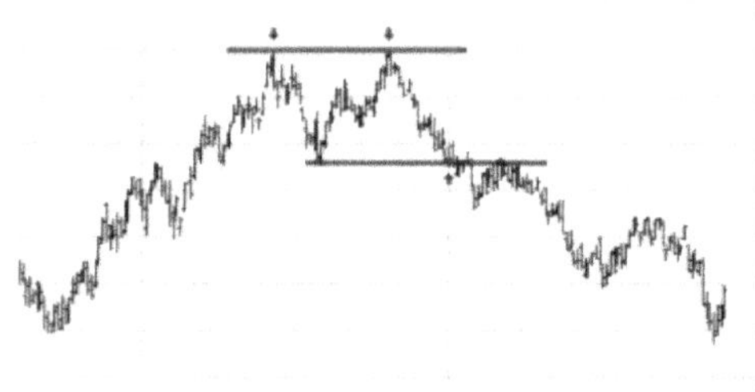

The entry signal in a Double Tops pattern is when the support level is violated. The price projection can be obtained by calculating the distance from the support level created from the retracement of the first peak and subtracting it from the point at which the support level was broken.

The entry signal in a Double Bottoms pattern is when the support level is violated. The price projection can be obtained by calculating the distance from the resistance level between the two dips and adding it to the point at which the resistance level was broken.

2. **Triple Tops & Bottoms.** These patterns are similar to the Double Tops & Bottoms pattern except that here the verification is through three tops and bottoms against two. Their interpretation is also similar.

3. **Head & Shoulders.** This is a reliable trend reversal pattern.

This pattern is usually seen in uptrends and is then called a Head & Shoulder Top pattern, but they may also appear in downtrends and then called Head & Shoulder Bottom pattern.

This is how a Head and Shoulder pattern looks like.

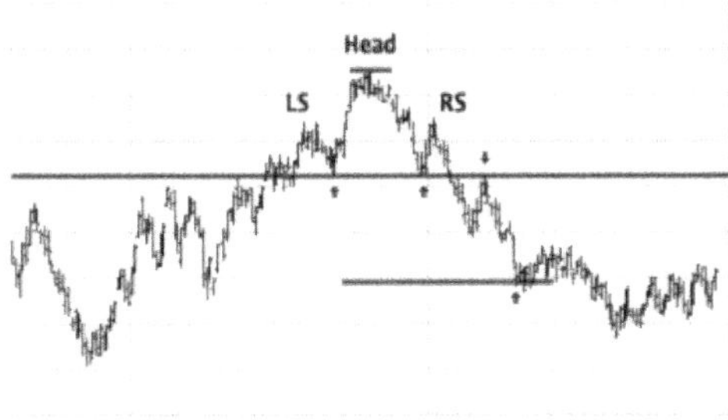

A Head & Shoulder Top is formed when a higher high is followed by a lower high resulting in three peaks where the centre peak is highest. The entry signal to sell is when the neckline is broken on the downside. Price projection is obtained by measuring the height of the centre peak to the neckline and subtracting it from the neckline at the point of breakout.

The Head & Shoulder Bottom is just the reverse of the Head & Shoulder Top pattern. It is formed when a higher low is followed by a lower low resulting in three dips where the centre dip is lowest. The entry signal to buy is when the neckline is broken on the upside. Price projection is obtained by measuring the height of the centre dip to the neckline and adding it to the neckline at the point of breakout.

4. **Rounding Bottom Pattern.** This is also called the Saucer Pattern. This pattern is formed during very long periods that may extend from several months to several years.

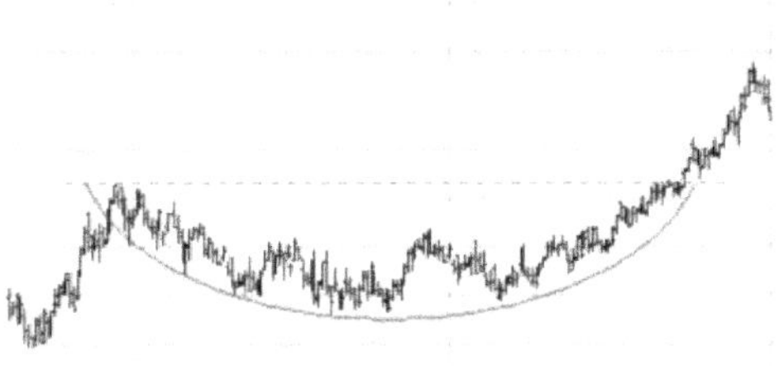

Since this pattern takes a long time to form it is difficult to identify.

16 RISK TO REWARD RATIO

Risk to Reward Ratio is used by investors and traders to assess the prospective reward they can earn for every rupee they risk on their investment. Let us say, that for a particular investment the risk to reward ratio is 1:5, then it means that the investor is willing to risk every rupee for a prospect to gain rupees five. Many strategists plan for a 1:3 Risk to Reward Ratio but this depends on the type of trade one wishes to execute, and it could be as low as 1:1.

Traders use stop loss to minimise losses and manage their investment by focussing on the Risk to Reward Ratio.

Let us understand this with an example. A trader wishes to buy 100 shares of a particular stock at a price of Rs 20 per share, places his stop loss at Rs 18 per share, and assumes that the stock would touch Rs 30 in a few days. Here, the trader is willing to take a risk of losing Rs 5 per share to make a potential gain of Rs 10 per share. Therefore, the Risk to Reward Ratio in this case would be $5/10 = 1:2$.

In the same example, if the trader puts his stop loss at Rs 18, rest remaining unchanged, he has reduced his risk to Rs 2 per share from Rs 5 earlier. The Risk to Reward Ratio now stands at $2/10 = 1:5$. The trader has the potential to get a better reward with less gain but his probability of achieving this trade has also reduced as the stop loss is too close to the entry price and might get triggered before it reaches its target price of Rs 30.

Risk to Reward Ratio is set by traders based on their risk appetite and understanding the current trend. Aggressive traders take up trades with 1 RRR, that is they risk Re 1 for every Re 1 of reward. Ultra-cautious traders may assume a 2 RRR, that is they risk Re 1 for every Rs 2 gain. Whatever RRR you plan, be ready to quit a trade that has gone wrong and look for another opportunity.

17 PICKING WINNING STOCKS FOR TRADING

"Successful investors are opportunistic and optimistic ones"

Rakesh Jhunjhunwala

There are about 6,000 stocks listed on the Bombay Stock Exchange and about 2,000 listed on the National Stock Exchange. It is not possible to scan all the listed stocks daily by individual investors or traders. Therefore, you need to select a few stocks from the huge numbers that exist, so that you can manage well. If you find this to be a difficult task, it may be best to stick to the 30 stocks that make up the Sensex or the 50 stocks that are in the Nifty basket. In case you decide to pick stocks outside of Sensex or Nifty make sure that the stock is in the EQ segment as only stocks in this segment can be day traded. In addition, see that the stock has adequate liquidity.

If you are opting to trade in stocks, you will have to visit each of your stocks daily to see emerging patterns. This is done by inspecting 3 to 4 candlesticks of each stock. Short list a few, generally 3 or 4, that interest you for detailed analysis as per the check list mentioned above.

PREPARATION OF A CHECK LIST

We have studied all the important indicators an investor or trader needs to know. It is a good idea to take help of a check list to ensure that nothing is missed out before taking a trading call. A suggested check list is shown below:

1. Has the stock formed a recognisable candlestick pattern?

    a. If the answer is yes, then which candlestick pattern is it?

    b. What are the inferences from the candlestick pattern?

2. Check the Support and Resistance levels. Place your stop loss around the Support or Resistance levels.

    a. For Long Trades, the low of a pattern should be around the Support level

    b. For Short Trades, the high of a pattern should be around the Resistance level

3. Check Volumes. Buy or Sell only on days when volumes are above the average traded volumes.

4. Look at the Dow theory indicators to confirm market phase and trend

    a. Which phase is the market in?

    b. Which trend is the market in?

    c. Are there any recognisable Dow patterns seen?

    d. What inferences the pattern suggests?

5. If the Dow indicators are in tune with the findings of your previous steps, one to three, then scale the trade higher. If the Dow indicators are not in tune with your previous steps, then go ahead with the original plan that you have arrived at after analysing steps one to three.

6. Fix your Risk to Reward Ratio. Complete beginners should fix this ratio as high as possible for being on a safer side, active traders can fix their ratios at least 1:5.

Once you finish detailed analysis you may be left with one or two trades that may interest you. However, there will be days when you may not have any worthwhile trades to make.

If you use the above check list, the chances of your trade going wrong will reduce tremendously. However, your success depends entirely on how you interpret the data.

By now you would have noticed that trading is not an easy task. It requires understanding, skill, time and total involvement. Professional traders are equipped with sophisticated charting software and have data feeds from vendors to assist them. All this comes at a cost. If you are short on any of these, my advice to retail investors is to remain away from trading. Your interests are best served by being a long-term investor.

While trading you are pitted against professionals, they can gain only when someone loses. You should not be amongst them.

18 TAX IMPLICATIONS ON SELLING STOCKS

"Investment is most successful when it is most business-like

Ben Graham

When you sell any asset which generates profit, the profit is liable to Capital Gains Tax. The asset can be in the form of shares, mutual funds, bonds, debentures, real estate, etc.

Capital Gains are classified under short term gains or long-term gains. Let us understand when short term gains apply and when long term gains apply as both have to satisfy some conditions and are taxed at different rates.

Short Term Capital Gains

Following assets when sold within one year of purchase will qualify as short-term capital gains:

1. Equity or preference shares of a company listed on stock exchanges.

2. Units of an equity oriented mutual fund.

3. Units of UTI quoted or not quoted.

4. Securities like bonds, debentures, etc which are listed on stock exchanges.

5. Zero coupon bonds quoted or not quoted.

If any property is sold within a period of 2 years after purchase, the profits qualify for short term gains. There is no tax when property is inherited but it will attract tax when sold. Sale of agricultural land does not qualify for short term capital gains.

In case of debt mutual funds, if these are sold within a period of 3 years, the profits are added into your income and taxed as per your tax slabs.

Calculation of Short-Term Capital Gains (STCG)

The calculation of short-term gains is simple. From the sale consideration, deduct costs of acquisition, transfer and improvement to arrive at the value of short-term capital gains.

The current rate at which short term capital gains are taxed is 15%. Only those assets will qualify where Securities Transaction Tax (STT) has been paid.

Long Term Capital Gains (LTCG)

Any asset that is sold beyond the periods listed under short term capital gains as explained above, the profits would qualify for long term capital gains.

In case of debt mutual funds, if these are sold after a period of 3 years from purchase, the profits qualify as long-term capital gains.

Agricultural land when sold, the profits qualify as long-term capital gains.

Calculation of Long-Term Capital Gains on Sale of Equity Products

For calculating long term capital gains on profits generated on sale of equity products, following needs to be considered:

1. Full sale consideration

2. Acquisition cost

3. Fair market value as on 31 Jan 2018 if asset purchased before this date
4. Brokerage expenses

Till the year 2017-18, there was no long-term capital gain tax on equities. LTCG tax was introduced during the Budget speech in 2018. So, to provide protection to equities purchased before this announcement, the government also allowed consideration of the asset value as on 31 Jan 2018. To understand this clearly, let us consider a few examples covering different scenarios.

Scenario A. Let us assume a person bought shares worth Rs 25,000 on 15 Sep 2016, and sold them for Rs 40,000 on 20 Oct 2019, and the fair value of the asset as on 31 Jan 2018 was Rs 30,000. In this case, the acquisition cost of Rs 25,000 is less than the fair market value of Rs 30,000, the cost of acquisition will be taken as Rs 30,000. Long term capital gains would then be Rs (40000-30000) which works out to Rs 10,500.

Scenario B. Let us assume a person bought shares worth Rs 25,000 on 15 Sep 2016, and sold them for Rs 28,000 on 20 Oct 2019, and the fair value of the asset as on 31 Jan 2018 was Rs 30,000. In this case also, the acquisition cost of Rs 25,000 is less than the fair market price of Rs 30,000 but the sale price of Rs 28,000 is also less than the fair market price of Rs 30,000. Here, the cost of acquisition will be taken as Rs 28,000. Hence there would be no capital gains.

Scenario C. Let us assume a person bought shares worth Rs 25,000 on 15 Sep 2016, and sold them for Rs 40,000 on 20 Oct 2019, and the fair value of the asset as on 31 Jan 2018 was Rs 20,000. In this case, the acquisition cost of Rs 25,000 is more than the fair market value of Rs 20,000. Here cost of acquisition will be Rs 25,000 and LTCG will be Rs (40000-25000) which works out to Rs 15,000.

Scenario D. Let us assume a person bought shares worth Rs 25,000 on 15 Sep 2016 and sold them for Rs 20,000 after paying a brokerage of Rs 500 on 20 Oct 2019, and the fair value of the asset as on 31 Jan 2018 was Rs 30,000. In this case, the acquisition cost of Rs 25,000 is less than the fair market value of Rs 30,000 and sale price of Rs 20,000 is also less than the fair market price, cost of acquisition will be Rs 25,000. Here there is a loss of LTCG of Rs (20000-25000) which works out to Rs 5,000.

Scenario E. Assume a person bought shares worth Rs 25,000 on 15 Apr 2018 and sold them for Rs 40,000 on 20 Oct 2019. In this case, the shares were acquired after 31 Jan 2018, so fair value as on 31 Jan does not apply. The LTCG is straight forward, Rs (40000-25000) which is Rs 15,000.

In all the above cases, you can deduct any expense like brokerage towards transfer. However, STT cannot be deducted as transfer expense.

You must have noticed that there is no application of indexation on sale of equity assets.

Calculation of Long-Term Capital Gains on Sale of Property or Debt Funds

Calculation of long-term capital gains is a little more complex but not difficult.

For calculating long term capital gains, you need to know the following:

1. Full sale consideration

2. Indexed cost of acquisition

3. Indexed cost of improvements, if any

4. Transfer costs

Cost inflation index (CII) is announced by the government each financial year. Values of these indices relevant to year of purchase and year of sale are used to calculate indexed costs. Historical values are available on websites.

The financial year 2001-02 has been taken as base year for cost inflation index. In case you have purchased an asset before this year, then you need to take higher of acquisition cost or fair price value as on 1st Apr 2001 and thereafter consider the indexation cost.

Let us understand the calculations of long-term capital gains based on an example for more clarity. Assume an asset was purchased in the year 2010-11 for Rs 10,00,000 and sold in the year 2018-19 for Rs 25,00,000 after spending Rs 1,00,000 on brokerage and another Rs 50,000 on improvement during the year 2015-16.

Firstly, we will find the cost inflation index for financial years 2010-11, 2015-16 and 2018-19 which are 167, 254 and 280 respectively.

We know the full sale consideration as Rs 25,00,000.

The indexed cost of acquisition is product of CII value of sale year and acquisition cost divided by CII of value of acquisition year. In this case, it would be (280x1000000)/167 which works out to Rs 16,76,647.

Similarly, we will find the indexed cost of improvements. In this case, it would be (280x50000)/254 which works out to Rs 55,118.

Cost of transfer is Rs 1,00,000.

Long Term Capital Gains in this case would be Rs 2500000-(1676647+55118+100000) which works out to Rs 6,68,235.

If the underlying asset is an equity-based product, then the rate at which long term capital gains are taxed is 10%. However, there is no tax if the gains are less than Rs 1,00,000.

If the underlying asset is a debt instrument or property, then the rate is 20% with indexation and 10% without indexation.

Expenses incurred on STT cannot be added to cost of transfer while calculating short- and long-term capital gains.

Short- & Long-Term Capital Losses

It is not always possible to make profits, you could incur losses as well. Losses can also be accounted as short or long term.

These losses cannot be adjusted against any other income gains. They can be set off within the capital gains head only.

Long term capital losses can only be set off against long term capital gains only.

However, short term capital losses can be set off against long- or short-term capital gains.

In case you are not able to adjust your losses in the year they occur, you can carry forward these losses for next 8 years.

These losses can be carried forward only if you have filed your tax returns before the due date. If you file your return after the due date, this benefit is denied. So, make sure you file your return in time.

How to Reduce the Impact of Short- & Long-Term Capital Gains

We know that short term capital losses can be set off against long- or short-term gains. So, in case you have made short- or long-term capital gains, then you can plan to sell a few of your stocks that are in loss just before the deadline of 31st Mar in that year thus adjusting this loss against your gains. You may buy the same or other stocks immediately after 1st Apr.

Long term capital gains on equity upto Rs 1,00,000 are exempted from long term capital tax. It may also be a good idea to take profits off the table from time to time to take advantage of this or else the gains over time may get larger and larger on which you will have to pay more tax.

Tax on Stock Dividends

From FY 2020-21 onwards, dividends will be treated as income and taxed as per your applicable tax slabs. The dividend distribution tax which the companies were paying earlier at 15% is no longer there. Therefore, if you are in the top tax bracket, your outgo has increased, and if you are in the lower tax slab or not liable to tax you get benefited.

Domestic companies are liable to withhold tax at the rate of 10% if the dividend income paid to resident individuals is more than Rs 5,000. The withheld tax will reflect in your Form 26AS statement.

As a temporary relief because of Covid-19, the companies will withhold tax at a rate of 7.5% for dividends received during FY 2020-21.

19 THE JOY OF GIVING BACK

"If you always give, you will always have"

Chinese Proverb

We all feel happy when we receive gifts. Should we then not give this happiness to people who are not as privileged as you? By giving you spread happiness and get joy in return.

India is the world's largest democracy, and the fifth largest economy by nominal GDP and the third largest in purchasing power parity. We have a growing middle-class population. This is good news. However, on the per capita income basis, India ranks 142 by nominal GDP and 124 on purchasing power parity. This is not good news.

There are several social and economic issues that plague our nation. There is still a large population that is poor, uneducated, mal nourished, unemployed and exploited. Many of them lack basic facilities of hygiene, sanitation, healthcare and education. The government alone cannot solve all the problems we face. As individuals, can we do something? I think we certainly can do many things to improve the quality of life of our fellow citizens no matter how small our effort is.

Giving is not restricted to giving money alone. There are many ways of giving happiness. A simple way could be by spending time with the old or sick or orphans. Even volunteering to teach poor children, run on errands for an old person in your neighborhood or helping people fill up their tax returns or calling up people who are lonely, sick or old are all acts of giving. Providing emotional support or paying a compliment or even giving a smile to strangers are yet other ways. So, you see there are several ways of giving and not limited to giving money.

Giving makes us richer. You don't have to be super rich to give. I know of many people with limited means who have given their time, knowledge, wisdom, compassion or wealth without anything in return.

Remember to be humble while giving and give without expecting anything in return. Never ever remind a person of what you gave him or her. If you do so, then your act doesn't qualify under giving as you have attached a motive to it.

'Charity begins at home' is an old saying. Start helping your own brothers or sisters who are less fortunate than you, or even your maid or driver. The joy you will get will be immense. When you give happiness to others, you get more happiness in return.

When you give, you get a new high. Your self-esteem grows, makes you more compassionate. Your personal worries start appearing insignificant when you listen to miseries of others. You become stronger.

Teach your children the merits of sharing and giving so that they become better social citizens.

Many religions advocate giving a percentage of your earnings to charity. Even scientists and psychologists tell us that people who give are happier than those who don't. If you are happy, your mind is peaceful, and you live longer.

In India, Azim Premji the founder chairman of Wipro has donated Rs 7,904 crores for education, followed by Shiv Nadar the founder chairman of HCL Technologies, Mukesh Ambani the Chairman of Reliance Industries, Kumaramangalam Birla the chairman of Aditya Birla Group, and Anil Agarwal the chairman of Vedanta Group who have donated Rs 795 crores for education, Rs 458 crores for disaster relief, Rs276 crores for education and Rs 215 crores for healthcare respectively.

There are several women entrepreneurs like Sudha Murthy, Kiran

Mazumdar-Shaw, Anu Aga who are working on several social causes.

There are many several lesser-known names who are donating and working for the betterment of society and the nation. One must read their stories for inspiration.

Donations to certain charities qualify for tax exemption under Sec 80G of the Income Tax Act.

On your part, give as much as you can, in any way you can. You will feel happy and blessed.

ABOUT THE AUTHOR

An engineer by profession, the author has held senior positions in the armed forces and the corporate world. He has been watching & investing successfully in stock markets for more than three decades.

This is his second book on investing. The first one, 'BE YOUR OWN FINANCIAL ADVISOR' introduced the reader to the various investment avenues available, how to create a financial plan based on your goals and risk profile, save on taxes, protect investments and the importance of a succession plan.

Apart from being an author and immensely admired by friends and colleagues, he is a keen photographer and a globe trotter. His other book, 'TRAVEL THE WORLD ON YOUR OWN' explains how one can create travel itineraries to dream destinations and obtain visas easily. You will be richer if you implement his many tried cost saving tricks.

9 798721 678417